THE URGE TO COLLECT

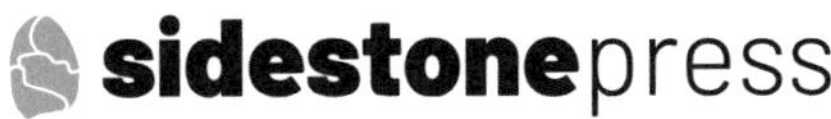

THE URGE TO COLLECT

MOTIVES, OBSESSIONS AND TENSIONS

HOLLY **O'FARRELL** AND PIETER **TER KEURS** (EDS)

Published by Sidestone Press, Leiden
www.sidestone.com

Lay-out & cover design: Sidestone Press
Photograph cover: Red Drawing Room, Waddesdon Manor.
Photo: Waddesdon Image Library, John Bigelow Taylor.

ISBN 978-94-6426-230-8 (softcover)
ISBN 978-94-6426-231-5 (hardcover)
ISBN 978-94-6426-232-2 (PDF e-book)

DOI: 10.59641/l02554ox

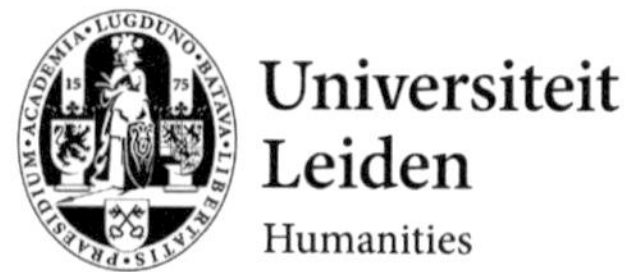

Contents

Foreword: The Urge to Collect

The phenomenon of collecting is as fascinating as it is complex. In a way, we are all collectors. Whether it concerns furniture for our living rooms, match boxes or expensive art, we all want to create a pleasant and familiar environment to shelter from the outside world or just to feel secure and comfortable as antidote for a busy life full of stress. For many of us, collecting helps to provide these sensations.

Collecting can be a relaxing activity, but it can also be stressful. To add to the collection leads to a sense of satisfaction, but when one does not succeed to obtain a desired object frustration is often the result. Obsessive collectors lose sight of daily-life, reality, may become socially unpleasant people and sometimes do not take ethical considerations very seriously. In these cases, the urge to collect has taken the reins and an individual may be consumed by the compulsion.

Collecting, in whatever form, is however always a clear expression of the complex relationship between human beings and things. It is a most clear example of how people relate to their external world and are trying to cope with it.

Why do we collect? Where does the urge to collect come from? This book explores the phenomenon of collecting in various contexts. Collecting is an illustration of a strong human-thing entanglement. It can be caused by psychological incentives that are deeply rooted in human doubts and anxieties. It is also related to building a pleasant, unthreatening, and even paradisiacal, environment to compensate for the uncertainties of everyday life. Collecting is a much more profound human impulse and coping mechanism than has generally been acknowledged by collectors and those studying the phenomenon. This book examines some examples of this phenomenon of collecting and the stimuli behind the activity.

The chapters in this book range from psychological perspectives in the Habsburg empire to Rococo collecting in France, from a fanatic English book collector to a $16^{th}/17^{th}$ century encyclopedic Dutch collector. And finally the fascinating story of Baron Edmond de Rothschild's boxes, illustrating how collecting often exceeds the gathering of objects to include the packaging and presentation of the treasures as well.

The contributions to this book were first presented as papers at the seminar "The Psychology of Collecting" on 20 April 2022, organized by the Interdisciplinary Research Group "Museums, Collections and Society" of Leiden University, Netherlands.

Holly O'Farrell
Pieter ter Keurs

The Urge to Collect: An Introduction

Pieter ter Keurs, Leiden University

Where does the urge to collect come from? What are the explicit or underlying reasons for gathering large amount of objects? In collecting, particularly in compulsive collecting there is a strong fusion between object and collector, the object and the subject. The attraction between what is collected and the collector is a key issue here, and this attraction is to a large extent what the philosopher Arthur Schopenhauer would call an irrational force.[1] Indeed, many collectors cannot verbalize why they collect, often very fanatically. People often can't reason why they want certain objects in their vicinity and why they want to touch them.

In specialized literature on collecting it is apparent that the phenomenon is very complex, but some common characteristics can be identified. The German psychoanalyst Peter Subkowski wrote:

> There is always a close and mostly unconscious relationship between the concrete object of collection and an individual's life history.[2]

The French philosopher and sociologist Jean Baudrillard described collecting as a:

> ultimate neurotic defence against the reality of the fear-inspiring passage of time, ending in one's inevitable death.[3]

---

1 Schopenhauer identified the "Will" as an irrational driving force behind life. The "Will" is, however, also present in non-human nature, such as animals, plants and material objects. See Schopenhauer's main work: *Die Welt als Wille und Vorstelling*, 1819.

2 Peter Subkowski, "On the psychodynamics of collecting," *The International Journal of Psychoanalysis*, 87 (2006), 383-401, 386.

3 Jean Baudrillard, *Le système des objects* (Paris: Gallimard, 1968).

So, the link with someone's individual life history is important, as well as feelings of uncertainty towards life itself.

By collecting large amounts of objects, the collector tries to slow down the passage of time and make it controllable. In doing so, the collector aims to create a perfect world, as a counterbalance to the imperfect, chaotic and uncertain outside world. Collectors often find a sense of security in collecting, a security they lack elsewhere. Being busy with processes of collecting, expanding, organizing, appreciating, creates security and provides pleasure. A serious collector enjoys his collection intensely. And this immediately shows an important usefulness of collecting: enjoying it and having a pleasant, safe feeling about it.

This pursuit of perfection in an imperfect world can, however, also be a form of pathology. Collectors can use collecting as a means of compensating for a loss, trauma, or unconscious desire. There may also be a perverse desire. The examples of collectors with psychological problems are fascinating to read. They are largely about the human-things entanglement and they give a good idea of why collectors can be so fanatical. Arranging a collection and creating an ideal world at home are clearly visible among many collectors as means to make uncertainty and conscious or unconscious fears bearable.

Not all collectors have a psychological problem. There are, of course, also a large number of collectors with stable, less eccentric personalities, but even among those collectors the urge to own objects, to surround themselves with them and to create a pleasant, confidential world is strong and often uncontrollable. The examples given below will illustrate the psychological dimension of collecting, including deeply rooted feelings of uncertainty and a striving for an ideal world.

The pathological collector

In the early 1990s, when I was a newly appointed curator at the National Museum of Ethnology in Leiden, I first met a fanatical collector of Asian art, living in an eastern region of the Netherlands. Let me just call him Mr. X here. From the first moment it was clear that I was dealing with a very driven man, but also someone who could be quite stubborn, self-absorbed and socially not very pleasant. At the same time, he sought contact with specialists with whom he could discuss his passion. Incidentally, those discussions were more of a monologue on his part than a real exchange of ideas. That is not an uncommon phenomenon. Avid collectors often seek contact with people who share a passionate interest in certain objects, and those contacts are much more than superficial, everyday conversations. The psychoanalyst Werner Muensterberger sees this as looking for something that the collector missed in his youth, for example a father figure.[4] The collector's collection is then the pretext

4 See, for example, Werner Muensterberger, *Collecting: An unruly passion* (Princeton: Princeton Legacy Library, 1994), 82.

for entering into a relationship, because it is a subject that can be discussed in a supposedly neutral and knowledgeable manner. The attention that the expert gives to the collector functions as a replacement for a lack, it helps the collector to make sense of life. After all, for some people collecting is life itself, collecting is all there is. This makes a fanatical collector a socially inappropriate and sometimes unpleasant person. Even with one's own immediate family, relationships can be difficult. Mr. X's house was cluttered with objects, much to the chagrin of his wife and children. The collection had become more important than his own family life. When he passed away, the family wanted to get rid of the collection as quickly as possible. Everything had to be sold quickly, otherwise it would end up in the bin.

I never became a father figure to Mr. X. I was too young for that and my kind of knowledge about meanings of objects and collecting contexts did not interest him. He mainly wanted to talk about patina and the aesthetics of the object. He was a genuine specialist in these area and that made him feel at home.

That collecting can take on pathological forms is also clearly visible in the out of control collecting activities of Sir Thomas Phillips (1792-1872).[5] His most famous statement is: "I wish to have ONE COPY OF EVERY BOOK IN THE WORLD!!!".[6] When he made this statement he was already an old man and it was common knowledge that he was ill-tempered, despotic and without any sense of compassion for other people. He knew how to use people to satisfy his urge to collect, but then dropped them again with the greatest of ease. Eventually, despite his wealth, he became a poor bill payer and did not care if others went bankrupt as a result. His own family also suffered. For example, his wife barely received an inheritance after his death. And the house that he wanted to leave to his daughter he had purposely not maintained because he did not like his son-in-law.

When Thomas Phillips decided to move in 1863, against his wife's wishes, it took him nine months, 103 wagonloads, 230 horses and 160 men to transfer his collection.[7] By the end of his life he owned about twenty thousand manuscripts and thirty thousand printed books. His fanaticism knew no bounds and his very selfish dealings with others made him an unpleasant person. The only people he got along with reasonably well were learned specialists. As with Mr. X mentioned above, Phillips was well connected with some connoisseurs towards the end of his life. His dealings with specialists could be very amiable and some testify to a friendly atmosphere. However, almost everyone who came to Phillips's house described the miserable state of the house and the horribly sloppy way in which the collection was managed. Sir Frederic Madden, curator of manuscripts at the British Museum, described the state of the collection as "miserable".

---

5 Muensterberger, *Collecting*, 73-100.

6 Muensterberger, *Collecting*, 74.

7 Muensterberger, *Collecting*, 75.

> Every room is filled with heaps of papers, MSS, books, charters, packages & other things, lying in heaps under your feet, piled upon tables, beds, chairs, ladders, &c., &c. and in every room, piles of huge boxes, up to the ceiling, containing even more valuable volumes! It is quite sickening! ... The windows of the house are never opened, and the close confined air & smell of the paper & MSS is almost unbearable.[8]

Sir Thomas Phillips was an disagreeable, socially maladjusted, mentally ill man. But what was the origin of this abnormal behaviour? Werner Muensterberger attempts an explanation. As described above, the fact that a collector seeks a good relationship with specialists may indicate the lack of a father figure, but a feeling of loss can go much further than that. There was more going on with Phillips. Although he also had a bad relationship with his father, one of the many people of the time who recently became very rich, he had missed much more in his youth. Sir Thomas was the son of a 21-year-old servant of his father, Hannah Walton. Thomas' father was not married and thus had no legitimate children, but with the birth of his illegitimate son he realized that he now had a potential heir. He adopted Thomas and Hannah Walton had to disappear. So, the son was not raised by a mother. He hardly knew his mother, although they occasionally kept in touch by letter. There is no evidence that another woman ever played a part in his upbringing. Such an origin must have caused a lot of tension for young Thomas. For a long time he was forbidden to communicate with his mother and he felt all his life that he could not speak openly about his origins.[9]

Apart from this complex family origin, Phillips was wealthy, but not a member of the nobility and therefore had no clear status in the English class society of the time. He was a "new rich" and the old nobility looked down on him. In Jane Austen's novel *Pride and Prejudice*, such a situation is succinctly portrayed in Mr. Bingley who was rich, but whose father was a just a shopkeeper. Elisabeth Bennett's aunt and uncle had a house in London and were in a comfortable financial position, but their London house was in Cheapside and that was not good enough for the real elite.

The uncertainty of the 'newly rich' must also have fuelled Thomas Phillips' collecting passion to a large extent. He frantically tried to be accepted by the people who mattered, to fit in, to achieve an accepted position and corresponding status. And of course, that didn't work out well. To compensate for his uncertain and controversial past, he started collecting, in order to be able to distinguish himself in one way or another. We often see this multiple lack, which originated in a flawed past, among fanatical collectors, especially when it concerns people who are self-made, have recently become rich, but have no relationship with the traditional elite. Scientists are probably more flexible, out of a certain scientific

8 Muensterberger, *Collecting*, 75.

9 Muensterberger, *Collecting*, 76-81.

curiosity, than representatives of the old nobility. The father figures can therefore be found there, not under barons, counts or dukes. And certainly not among kings and princes.

Phillips couldn't talk to anyone about his background. As a result, he had difficulty joining any social class (preferably, of course, the nobility) and had a strained relationship with the past. He was constantly nervously looking for something to hold onto in the past. Especially after the death of his father, when both parents have disappeared from his life, the collecting urge of Phillips Jr. takes on absurd forms. Perhaps this was a means for Sir Thomas to come to terms with the past in one way or another. The fact that he spent much more money than his father's substantial inheritance allowed didn't interest him. He frequently failed to pay his bills, a quality he had already demonstrated earlier in life.

Lack, order and the ideal world

Relatively few psychoanalytic studies have been done on collecting. Muensterberger's book *Collecting: An Unruly Passion* (1994) is one of the few works that does pay in-depth attention to the psychology of collecting. The German-Dutch Werner Muensterberger was born in 1913, in Hörde (now Dortmund). His father was German, his mother Dutch. He was raised bilingually and spent much of his childhood with his grandmother in Haarlem. During the Second World War he went into hiding in Amsterdam with the actress Elisabeth Andersen, with whom he also had an intimate relationship. After the war, Muensterberger emigrated to the United States, where he built up a thriving psychoanalytic practice. He made a name for himself as a therapist for celebrities such as Marlon Brando and James Dean.

Muensterberger was fascinated by the phenomenon of collecting all his life. He also collected himself and knew many great collectors personally. Because of his interest, he often had access to personal information and, as an equal, engaged in intense conversations about collectors' motives for fanatically getting into a particular type of collectible. His book is full of interesting examples, sometimes using fictitious names to protect the privacy of the collector.

Where does the relentless need to collect come from? How can we be so guided by the urge to possess that it transcends everything: work, family, social obligations and responsibilities. Muensterberger's main answer to this question is that collectors often want to shield and compensate for major doubts and uncertainties. A difficult relationship with the past plays an important role in this. We have already seen this with the example of Sir Thomas Phillips, but even without delving deep into someone's psychological past, we find clear examples of how the past can affect someone. The immensely wealthy American collector Nelson Rockefeller once told Muensterberger that he had no choice. His mother collected and his grandfather collected, so he had to follow in their footsteps. His remark "After all, the Medici's did it too" is also illustrative.

Nelson's son, Michael Rockefeller, would continue the tradition with his collecting activities in what was then Dutch New Guinea. His uncontrollable fanaticism would eventually lead to his death.[10]

The relationship with a flawed past also turned out to be the basis of the depression of Nick, one of Muensterberger's patients. At the first meeting between patient and therapist, Nick was 40 years old. He had a fascination with one very special object, but was also always looking for an even better object. If he had found and was able to acquire a better, more beautiful, more unique object, often at great financial sacrifice, Nick would be satisfied again until an even better one turned up. The earlier object was subsequently disposed of. The unrest that this constant search for 'even better' entailed was very problematic.

Nick's relationship with the dealer who supplied him became better in the course of time, when even better pieces became available, but also more complex. The man confirmed Nick in his opinions about objects and developed into a father figure. On the one hand this was pleasant for Nick, who turned out to need a supportive father figure, but on the other hand it confirmed him in his constant search for better pieces. Muensterberger claims that this development almost led to a paranoid attitude towards the whole outside world, an outside world that, like an all-demanding father, wanted better and better.

Not surprisingly, Nick had a domineering father, an army officer who was viewed with fear by the entire family. If Nick got an A on a paper at school, his father wouldn't compliment him. As a kick after he was told that it was not an A plus and therefore not good enough. This pursuit for an A plus has largely driven Nick's urge to collect. It was never enough and he still felt pressured by his father. After his father's death, he sought substitute father figures in the world of collectors and dealers. In the end, Nick's case was all about creating a place for himself in the world, but it wasn't until the trader/father figure in question moved, and Nick no longer had direct contact with him, that he realized that he had always mirrored his father's standards. The lack of paternal warmth and the occasional pat on the back had major consequences for son Nick for decades. And objects apparently play a major role in compensating (and at the same time masking) such a lack.

Creating a structure by organizing a collection is also a way of dealing with a chaotic outside world or a chaotic past. Muensterberger cites the German writer

---

10 Michael Rockefeller's disappearance in New Guinea was never resolved, resulting in a lively oral history in New Guinea as well as the Netherlands. Former Dutch civil servants and researchers in New Guinea portray Michael Rockefeller as a one-minded, somewhat headstrong person (personal communication). He focused primarily on collecting Asmat art. His collection is now in the Metropolitan Museum in New York.

Walter Benjamin (1892-1940) as an example. Benjamin was an avid collector of manuscripts, loose notes, clippings, etc. His archive formed the basis for the posthumously published Arcade work, an analysis of the emergence and functioning of the shopping arcades in Paris.[11] No less important is Benjamin's essay on his book collection, in which he describes unpacking his book collection.[12]

Walter Benjamin never had a permanent residence after his childhood in Berlin. His father had lost a lot of money in the 1930s, the crisis years, and was no longer able to support his son financially. A job in the university world was not an option for him, although he was a brilliant researcher. Only after his death did he become widely known as an original thinker. During his life, he just couldn't finish things. His fascination with the Parisian nineteenth-century shopping arcades knew no bounds, but a book on the subject was not published during his lifetime.

Benjamin lived off occasional writing assignments and radio appearances and the goodwill of friends. Usually he could stay in friends' houses or apartments, so it was very special if he could stay somewhere longer, for example in a summer house of friends. And then, when he could be somewhere for more than a few months, he could also unpack his book collection. He describes with noticeable pleasure the process of unpacking, organizing and thereby creating an ideal world, a world in which he felt at home and which made him forget the misery of time for a while. The beginning of his text is touching:

> I am unpacking my library. Yes, I am. The books are not yet on the shelves, not yet touched by the mild boredom of order. I cannot march up and down their ranks to pass them in review before a friendly audience. You need not fear any of that. Instead, I must ask you to join me in the disorder of crates ...[13]

For Benjamin, the process of collecting was probably as important as the things that were collected. He drew attention to what a collector actually does, how he touches an object with his hands, strokes it and how he observes it. And also how he structures his collection, to create order. By creating a structure, the collector creates an ideal world as a counterweight to the chaotic and often dangerous outside world. It is also as if he is looking through the objects to the distant past from which they come. Here too we see the importance of a bond with the past, but also of exceeding one's own lifespan. Collecting then acquires an eternal value, the collected collection retains its meaning even after the death of the owner. The collector then becomes a conduit for items of interest from one generation to the next. That was certainly the case with

---

11 Walter Benjamin, *The Arcades Project*, ed. Rolf Tiedemann (New York: Belknap Press, 2002).

12 Walter Benjamin, "Unpacking my Library. A Talk on Book Collecting," in *Illuminations, Essay and Reflections* New York: Schocken Books, 1969), 59-67.

13 Benjamin, "Unpacking my Library," 59.

Walter Benjamin. Generations of researchers have benefited from and built on his work and his archive.

A special element of Muensterberger's work is the use of ethnological knowledge in analyzing the phenomenon of collecting. Muensterberger himself collected art from Africa and Oceania and was very familiar with the relevant anthropological literature. He used this knowledge not only to interpret the objects, but also to support his psychological analyses. For example, the concept of *mana* is important for his way of analyzing. *Mana* is a Polynesian concept that stands for the power or the force of an object. *Mana* allows the object to be an active actor in a network of things and people.[14] This indicates that an object is not, as we in the West tend to believe, a dead object, but a living thing that influences the environment. This living nature of an object also often plays a major role for collectors. We see this in the loving way in which objects are touched or in the use of personal pronouns when talking about the objects. There is often an intimate relationship between the collector and the collected, such that many collectors are more interested in their collection than in social contacts with felow human beings. Objects become like people. This allows the collector to arrange and decorate the world as he sees fit.

Muensterberger noticed that many collectors spoke openly about a loss, a feeling of insecurity or a disappointment in their youth and about traumas they had experienced in their lives. Collecting can therefore have a therapeutic, beneficial effect on the collector, as long as it does not take on morbid forms.

Insecurity, fear and Mr. H.

Collectors often find a sense of security in collecting, a security they lack elsewhere. Working with the collection, expanding, organizing, appreciating, creates security and provides pleasure. A serious collector thoroughly enjoys his collection. And that immediately shows an important usefulness of collecting: enjoying it and having a pleasant, secure feeling about it. A psychological analysis of collecting is of no interest to many collectors because that is not what they care about. Many collectors don't want to understand what they are doing, they want to enjoy it.

Some psychologists discuss collecting in Freudian terms, such as the Oedipus complex, sexual frustrations, or castration anxiety. Collecting would then be a compensation for sexual frustrations and the collector withdraws into a world of objects created by himself, safely shielded from the dangers and uncertainties of the world outside. The German psychoanalyst Peter Subkowski is such a Freudian-minded psychologist, but one of his most fascinating examples is easy to understand even without reducing the urge to collect to sexual frustrations.

---

14 This idea aligns well with the influential works of Bruno Latour and Alfred Gell. These network and agency approaches developed around the same period in which Muensterberger wrote and published his book *Collecting: An Unruly Passion* (1994).

Subkowksi first makes it clear that he is not concerned with limiting or stopping collecting behaviour of his patients as a symptom of a disease, but with making it a subject of discussion and integrating it into daily life, just like our daily dealings with objects. Explaining compulsive collecting behaviour can already help a patient and subsequently learn to deal with social relationships that were previously experienced as problematic. An instructive example is Mr. H. This 40-year-old man approached Subkowksi with the question 'how do human relationships actually work'.[15] Apparently he had trouble with human relationships and was unable to sustain a relationship for long. For example, he was already divorced at that time and occasionally had major tantrums. He could, however, talk with devotion about his passion, collecting books about politics and his interest in important politicians and statesmen.[16]

The therapist soon learned that Mr. H. had experienced his grandmother and mother as very dominant. His father was anxious and shy. Both parental families had a working-class background and young H. had the heavy task of doing better and breaking out of the family environment. Poor performance in school was heavily blamed on him. He turned out to have dyslexia, but his mother explained his bad marks as stupidity. At the age of eleven he had to leave school because he "would not pass the exams anyway". Later, H. would finish school on his own and complete a good management education. He would also work as a successful and valued manager for a time. However, his real feelings remained under the surface. He identified with his father and felt lonely, anxious and insecure towards women. He admitted that he never fully trusted women in particular. At the age of 25, H. married, but he also struggled with the fact that he did not trust others, including his own wife, and therefore did not feel comfortable with them. This fundamental mistrust increasingly led to tantrums and eventually to a divorce.

Mr. H. had started collecting rare books on politics at an early age and as life became more and more difficult for him, he retreated and found solace in his career and in book buying. One of the reasons he sought help from a psychologist was that he feared his book mania would become uncontrollable. After his divorce, H. had withdrawn more and more into the world of his books. After a period of alcohol addiction, he took refuge in the books again. In Subkowski's waiting room, H. usually sat reading a book. Books gave him a sense of security, calmness and control over the world on the one hand and on the other hand he could show that he had indeed left his family's working-class past behind. Yet Mr. H. kept his therapist at a distance for a long time. It wasn't until they started analysing his dreams that it gradually became clearer. It goes too far to go into details here, but it was only when the dreams were connected to friendships from his youth that H. gained more understanding. School

15 Subkowski, *On the psychodynamics of collecting*, 396.

16 Subkowski, *On the psychodynamics of collecting*, 396-397.

friends never came to his house, because he lived in a working-class house and on those few occasions when he did feel a deep friendship for a schoolmate, homoerotic feelings could not be avoided in the conversations. Insight into all these things, which had long been consciously or unconsciously suppressed, acted as an eye-opener for H. In this way he could place his fanatical collecting practices in context: Not to stop it, but to turn it into something valuable, something useful for every day, normal life. Subkowski concludes that H. developed into a person who was more emotionally open, also to others, and who allowed himself to be influenced in a positive way by interactions with others. Just as his books could positively influence him, now other people could as well. Collecting remained his hobby, but less compulsive than before.

Before Mr. H. became a more balanced person, the therapist had six hundred sessions with him, with an average of four a week. Deep-lying problems and motivations are not easy to identify and when they eventually become visible, they must also be used in a positive way. Collecting is more than just a fun, harmless hobby. Collecting can lead to pathologic behaviour, but it can also offer comfort and satisfaction. Subkowski describes it as follows:

> ... collecting offers a way to console oneself for being left, give narcissistic validation and calm tempestuous emotions. It expresses a yearning for completeness and for a world which is to become perfectly shaped by way of the collection.[17]

17 Subkowski, *On the psychodynamics of collecting*, 387.

What Drives the Collector?

The Case of Rococo Collecting

Caroline van Eck

Introduction

The period from 1715 to 1770 in France is quite unique in the history of collecting, and offers several openings to rethink received ideas about the psychology of collecting. It began with the Régence following the death of Louis XIV in 1715, in which a new type of collector emerged, the wealthy private individual, who collected contemporary art as well as past masters. From the 1770s onwards collecting became part of a new, highly influential configuration of restoration, display, and the art trade. This new configuration was caused by the arrival on the market in Rome of vast numbers of Roman Imperial fragments, recently excavated at Tivoli and other sites, by Giovanni Battista Piranesi, Cardinal Albani, the Vatican, and British collectors. Piranesi was one of the major shapers of this new configuration, involved in excavations near Tivoli, as well the restoration, appropriation of these fragments into new works, display and sale of his finds. For these purposes he founded a Museo, in fact a display room, restoration studio and shop.[1] As in the collection of Cardinal Albani, who hosted Winckelmann when he wrote his *Geschichte der Kunst des Altertums* (1763), Piranesi's Museo functioned as a major laboratory where a new style of design, variously labelled *retour à l'antique* at the time, and subsequently neo-classicism in 20th-century art history, as well as new histories of Graeco-Roman

1 On Piranesi's activities as a restorer and dealer in antiquities see most recently Pierluigi Panza, *Museo Piranesi* (Geneva/Milan: Skira, 2017).

art were evolved. This new configuration was a major factor in the foundation of the Museo Pio-Clementino, one of the first modern art galleries.[2]

This part of the eighteenth century stands out in the history of collecting in France, because we can observe at quite close range very different collectors collecting the same kind of art works to different purposes. The rich banker Pierre Crozat, the grandson of a local merchant in Toulouse, but himself the administrator of the finances of Louis XIV, collected Italian and German Renaissance masters, but also contemporary artists, chief among them Antoine Watteau, a major creator of the Rococo. At the same time the Comtesse de la Verrue, a member of the highest ranks of the French aristocracy, also collected Watteau, as well as Van Dyck, Netherlandish Masters, and Rubens. Both collections created environments in which art could be seen and analysed, inspired major artists, and played a major role in the creation of the collections of what would become the Musée du Louvre. Both are also well documented, and this offers some material to reconsider the received opinion of the collector as an obsessive, if not a fetishist of art.

Why is collecting a problem?

There certainly are well-known cases of problematic behaviour by collectors in this period. There is the famous case of the British collector Charles Townley. When his London house came under attack during the Gordon riots in 1780, he took his favourite marble bust of Clytie with him, but decided to leave his wife at home, to face the danger of lynching by the riotous mob.[3] We could also cite the enormous sums paid by collectors for the antiquities restored by Piranesi -- candelabra, vases, tripods -- which surpassed the price of Graeco-Roman statuary, but in our eyes are of far less artistic value, and as we now know, in fact were bricolages, largely produced by Piranesi; they soon entered into a steep decline in

2 On the Roman art market in antiquities see Ilaria Bignamini and Clare Hornsby, *Digging and Dealing in Eighteenth-Century Rome* (New Haven and London: Yale University Press, 2004). For a general historical overview of the emergence of the art gallery see Krisztof Pomian, *Le musée, une histoire mondiale, 1. Du trésor au musée* (Paris: Gallimard, 2020), 464-522; on the origins of the Museo Pio-Clementino Jeffrey Collins, "Museo Pio-Clementino, Vatican City: Ideology and Aesthetics in the Age of the Grand Tour," in *The First Modern Museums of Art. The Birth of an Institution in 18th- and early 19th-century Europe*, edited by Carole Paul (Los Angeles: The J.Paul Getty Museum, 2012), 113-145; and Daniela Gallo, "Il Museo Clementino tra novità e tradizione," in Mario Rosa and Marina Colonna (eds.), *L'età di papa Clemente XIV* (Rome: Bulzoni, 2010), 237-258. On the emergence of neo-classicism as a style concept in the twentieth century see John Whiteley, "The Origin and the Concept of 'classique' in French Art Criticism,' *Journal of the Warburg and Courtauld Institutes* 39 (1976): 268-75; and Pascal Griener, "La 'Periode' comme entrave: Le 'néoclassicsme' après Wölfflin," *Perspective: La revue de l'INHA* 5 (2008): 653-62.

3 Ruth Guilding, *Owning the Past. Why the English Collected Antique Sculpture, 1640*-1840 (New Haven and London: Yale University Press, 2014), 221, 242-4. On other occasions he had also referred to the bust as 'his wife'. See Viccy Coltman, "Representation, Replication and Collecting in Charles Townley's Late Eighteenth-Century Library," *Art History* 29/2 (2006), 304-24, here p. 308.

appreciation from which they have not recovered. Similar cases from the end of the eighteenth century abound: from the very well-known account by Goethe of Sir William Hamilton fetishizing his wife by putting a picture frame around her when she performed her attitudes, to this far less famous anonymous view of the collector's fetishizing gaze, published c. 1800 in Paris.[4]

In France the best-documented case of problematic collector behaviour is probably that of the 17th-century cardinal and prime minister Mazarin. It was problematic in two ways: first, we know from the memoirs of Loménie de Brienne, another obsessive collector, how the cardinal, when he knew he was dying, went round his collection, taking leave of each art work, and telling his paintings, sculptures and tapestries how much he would miss them. He then died, surrounded by his favourite pieces. His son-in-law, who inherited the collection, then smashed many classical statues to pieces out of disgust with what he called the idolatry of his father-in-law, but also out of unease with the sexual attractiveness of these statues. Eventually many pieces would be saved by Louis XIV. Their finding shelter in his collection is celebrated in the famous anonymous *Plainte des statues*, in which the statues themselves become alive and tell of their woes and rescue.[5]

But these are isolated cases. As I have argued elsewhere, it is extremely rare before the nineteenth century to describe any engagement with art in the West in terms of fetishism. Probably the first to suggest that collecting art is a kind of fetishism was Johann Wolfgang von Goethe in his novella *Der Sammler und die Seinigen* of 1799.[6] The word 'collectionneur' is a nineteenth-century coinage, in contrast to the term 'amateur', 'curieux' or 'connoisseur' used in the eighteenth century. Major sources for eighteenth-century attitudes to collecting can be found in that century's invention, the portable auction and exhibition catalogue. The art dealer Edme Gersaint for instance imported the Dutch format of art and luxury goods auctions to Paris, and developed the portable auction catalogue as we know it now. In the prefaces to these catalogues he has much to say about the nature

---

4 Johann Wolfgang von Goethe, *Italienische Reise.* Edited by Andreas Beyer, Norbert Miller and Christof Thoenes (Munich: Carl Hanser, 1992): 258: 'Der alte Ritter hält das Licht dazu und hat mit ganzer Seele sich diesem Gegenstand ergeben' see also Karl August Böttiger, "Tischbein's Vasen, Lady Hamilton's Attitüden von Rehberg," *Journal des Luxus und der Mode* (February 1795): 58-85; and Andrei Pop, "Sympathetic Spectators: Henry Fuseli's Nightmare and Emma Hamilton's Attitudes," *Art History* 34 (2011), 934-957.

5 See Patrick Michel (ed.), *Mazarin, prince des collectionneurs. Les collections et l'ameublement du Cardinal Mazarin (1602-1661), histoire et analyse* (Paris: Réunion des Musées nationaux, 1999), 320-22 and Appendix B, 570-72; and Katherine Ibbett, "Who makes the statue speak? Louis XIV and the *Plainte des statues*," *Word and Image* 24/2008, 427-438, here p. 427.

6 Johann Wolfgang von Goethe, *Der Sammler und die Seinigen. Herausgegeben und mit einem Essay von Carrie Asman* (Amsterdam and Dresden: Verlag der Kunst, 1997); see also Caroline van Eck, *Art, Agency and Living Presence: From the Animated Image to the Excessive Object* (Munich: Degruyter, 2016), Chapter Six; Renata Schellenberger, "The Self and Other Things: Goethe the Collector," *Publications of the English Goethe Society* 81/3 (2012), 166-77.

and purpose of collecting, but it falls quite neatly into the terms of curiosity, connoisseurship and love of the arts.[7] In the nineteenth century authors would often contrast the disinterested love for the arts of the amateur with the financial, social or political motives of the collectionneur, who in this view has an abnormal psychological investment in 'the fact of material possession', as the collector and historian of collecting Gault de Saint-Germain observed in 1841.[8] The figure of the obsessive collector, who becomes a hoarder and fetishizes his collection, appears to emerge more fully in the nineteenth century, and as Tom Stammers has recently noted in his *The Purchase of the Past: Collecting Cultures in Post-Revolutionary France*, it appears mainly in literary, fictional accounts of collectors.[9] The image of the collectionneur as a solitary obsessive, capable of entertaining affective relations exclusively with objects, a freudian fetishist avant la lettre, is very much based on literary accounts of collectors, starting with Balzac's *Le Cousin Pons* (1847), continued with Flaubert's *Bouvard et Pécuchet*, documented in the diary of the Goncourt Brothers, and culminating in Huysmans *A Rebours*. In this perspective the Goncourt diary is particularly revealing, because it offers such a rich catalogue of what the Dutch author Voskuil called unsuccessful human interactions, particularly with women, iuxtaposed with instances where the brothers engage in very satisfying encounters with art works.[10] These look almost like exercises in displacement of affects from persons and life itself to images, for instance in their account of looking at Watteau's *Comédiens français* of c. 1720, now in the Metropolitan Museum [Figure 2.1]. In the entries for 1859 for instance two passages succeed each other at a brief interval that are illustrative of this role of art as a way of putting life at a remove: first, the brothers describe how Watteau's *Comédiens français* succeeds much better than an actual performance of a tragedy by Racine in showing what these tragedies were really like: 'rien ne la montre comme une image, cette gravure des *Comédiens français* de Watteau' ['Nothing shows it as well

7 See for instance his catalogue for the sale of the cabinet of Quentin de Lorangère (Paris: J. Barois, 1744), 2-3, as discussed in Kristel Smentek, *Mariette and the Science of the Connoisseur* (Farnham: Ashgate, 2014), 95-96.

8 Tom Stammers, *The Purchase of the Past: Collecting Cultures in Post-Revolutionary France* (Cambridge: Cambridge University Press, 2020), 27; the reference is to Gault de Saint-Germain's *Guide des amateurs de tableaux pour les écoles flamandes …* (Paris, 1841).

9 See e.g. Bernard Vouilloux, "Le discours sur la collection", Romantisme 1/2 (2001), 95-108, with important bibliography; Dominique Péty, *Poétique de la collection. Du document de l'historien au bibelot de l'esthète* (Paris: Presses Universitaires de Paris-Nanterre, 2010); Eva Bielecki, *The Collector in Nineteenth-Century French Literature. Representation, Identity, Knowledge* (Oxford etc: Peter Lang, 2012). For collecting of eighteenth-century art in the nineteenth century see Christoph M. Vogtherr, *Delicious Decadence: The Rediscovery of French Eighteenth-Century Painting in the Nineteenth Century* (Aldershot: Ashgate, 2014).

10 J.J. Voskuil, *Het Bureau*, 6 vols., Amsterdam: Van Oorschot, 1996-2000, *passim*.

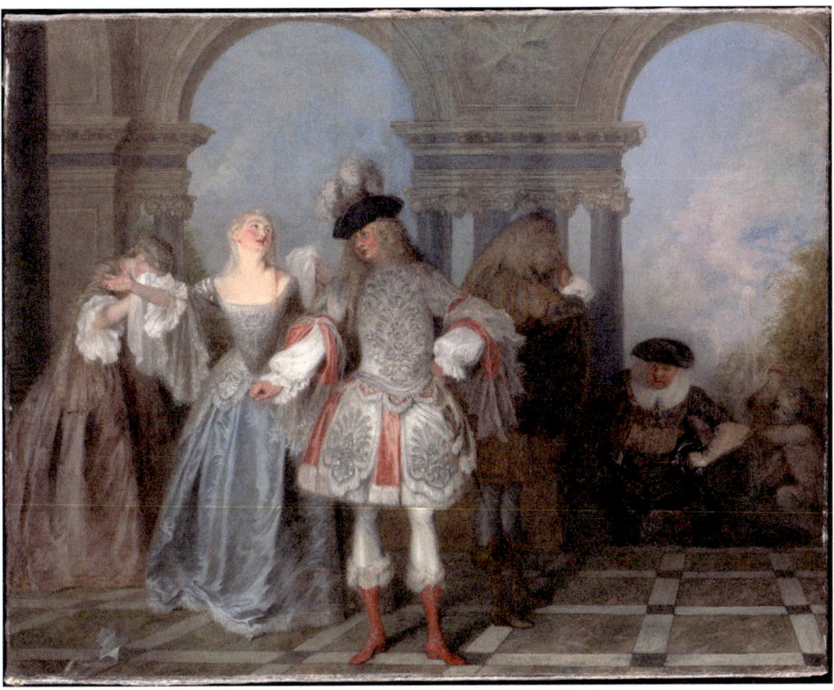

Figure 2.1: Antoine Watteau (1684-1721), Les Comédiens Français, c. 1720, oil on canvas, 57.2 x 73 cm (New York: Metropolitan Museum, The Jules Bache Collection, 1949).

as an image, this engraving of the *Comédiens français* de Watteau'].[11] A few months later they describe, or rather Jules describes, a night spent next to his sleeping mistress, in which he overhears her talking in her sleep. This is what he says:

> Oui, il y a comme une terreur à être penché sur ce corps, où tout semble éteint, et où la vie animale seule semble veiller, et à entendre ainsi le passé revenir ... ce mystère d'une pensée sans conscience, cette voix dans cette chambre noire, c'est quelque chose d'effrayant, comme un cadavre possédé par un rêve.[12]
>
> ['Yes, it is like a terror to bend over this body, in which all seems extinguished, and in which only animal life seems to be wakeful, and to hear in this manner the past come back ... this mystery of a thought without conscience, this voice in a black room, it is frightening, as a corpse possessed by a dream.']

11 Edmond and Jules de Goncourt, *Journal*, entry for May 8, quoted from the abridged edition by Jean-Louis Cabanès (Paris: Folio 2020), 128 -29.

12 Edmond et Jules de Goncourt, *Journal*, entry for September 3, 132.

Much is to be said about this suggestion that an image can create the sense of life better than a tragedy performed, and conversely, about the reduction of their living and breathing mistress, who speaks in her dreams, into a dead, animal body, bereft of humanity and conscience, a disembodied voice, a dead corpse. In a similar vein the great nineteenth-century collector Léopold Double, one of the founders of the concept of the period room, talked about his collection as his mistress, and felt that in collecting eighteenth-century art he somehow got in touch with the divine, Catholic Bourbon essence of France. Here, as Marjorie Garber observed in her article on collecting titled 'Overcoming Auction block', stories often seem to masquerade as objects.[13] And like Mazarin, Double died surrounded by his favourite objects.

So why is collecting a problem, as the Introduction to this collection of essays asks? At first sight, and this also seems to be the consensus in the literature, when the emotional engagement with the object, variously called object investment, or human-thing entanglement, or fetishism, takes over from consideration of the intrinsic interest of the object. The American pedagogue William Durost in 1932 already distinguished interest in intrinsic qualities (use, purpose, aesthetic qualities), which for him did not qualify collecting objects possessed of these qualities as collecting proper. For him a collection comes into being when objects are valued for the relation they bear to other objects or ideas, such as being one of a series, or a specimen of a class.[14] That distinction is the foundation for subsequent theorizing about the psychology of collecting. More recently Aristides called collecting 'an obsession organized'.[15] Psychologists such as Werner Muensterberger in his *Collecting: An Unruly Passion* (1994) have used Freud's theory of fetishism as paraphillia, the displacement of affections normally felt for humans onto objects.[16] Often this is combined with David Winnicott's theory of the transitional object, to develop an account of collecting that locates its origins and explains its intense drive by identifying a childhood trauma, and connecting this to phallic/narcistic personality traits. Here collecting is a compulsion meant to relieve the anxiety caused by childhood trauma.[17] As with Freud's account of fetishism, there

---

13 Marjorie Garber, "Overcoming Auction Block," *Critical Enquiry* 34/4 (1992), 74-84, quoted by Stammers, *The Purchase of the Past*, 234.

14 W. Durost, *Children's Collecting Activity Related to Social Factors* (New York, Bureau of Publications, Teachers' College, Columbia University, 1932), 10; quoted in Susan Pearce, *On Collecting. An Investigation into Collecting in the European Tradition* (London: Routledge 1995), 19.

15 N. Aristides, N., "Calm and Uncollected," *American Scholar*, 57/3 (1988): 327-36; quoted in Pearce, *On Collecting*, 20.

16 Sigmund Freud, *Drei Abhandlungen zur Sexualtheorie* (Vienna 1905); on the history of fetishism theories see Hartmut Böhme, *Fetischismus und Kultur. Eine andere Theorie der Moderne* (Reinbek bei Hamburg: Rowohlt Taschenbuch Verlag, 2006); Hartmut Böhme and Johannes Endres, *Der Code der Leidenschaften: Fetischismus in den Künsten* (Munich: Fink, 2010); and Van Eck, *Art, Agency and Living Presence*, Chapter Five. On Freud's own collecting see J. Forrester, "Collector, Naturalist, Surrealist," in *Despatches from the Freud Wars* (Cambridge, Mass.: MIT Press, 1997), 107-37.

17 See for instance David Winnicott, "Transitional Objects and Transitional Phenomena," *International Journal of Psycho-Analysis* 34/2 (1953); republished in idem, *Collected Papers: Through Pediatrics to Psycho-Analysis* (London: Tavistock Publications, 1958).

are two problems with this, often rehearsed: it is based on an outdated, male theory of child development and psychodynamics; and it has much to say about the psychology of the collector, but very little about the actual nature of the objects collected.

So if we leave aside these psycho-analytic accounts of the problematic aspects of collecting as represented in fiction, why is it a problem, and an interesting problem? I would argue for at least three reasons: one is that, after the previous stages of the history of collecting, described by Susan Pearce in her 1995 book *On Collecting* as, first a rather anecdotal history of individual collectors and their collections, next moving into a phase that concentrates on institutional and national developments, we now see, partly under the influence of the material turn, a new interest in collecting as a process because it offers such a rich field of cases of human-thing entanglement, documents the agency of objects, and affords major opportunities to write the biographies of objects. My own book on Piranesi's late candelabra is a case in point.[18]

In the second place, and this is perhaps mainly a problem for art historians, it is clear that in collecting there is always a tension between intrinsic qualities if not values of objects and the attribution of qualities and values to them when a collector makes them part of a collection. For the art historian the intrinsic value can take many shapes, from documenting an artist's manner of working, dating and attributing art works, to intrinsic artistic or aesthetic values, in short beauty. As we have seen, the collector can endow art works with all kinds of affects or emotional functions, but also reduce them to elements of a series. To speak from my own experience, my first acquisition of a work by the Dutch abstract expressionist Bram van Velde felt like a unique act, almost as if I had acquired a new member of the family, but now that I have five of them, concerns of completion and seriality, and considerations of where they stand in his artistic career, or even memories of that first art buy, take over. Since this intrinsic aspect can take so many forms, the wider set of relations within a collection, or all the ways in which a collector can engage with, and be affected by her collectiion can be very difficult to define or to theorize.

In the third place, the history of collecting has become highly politicized. There are the obvious issues of ownership and restitution, but as the recent book by Tom Stammers, as well as James McAuley's *The House of Fragile Things*, a study of Jewish collectors of French eighteenth-century art, both show, nineteenth- and early twentieth-century French collectors had highly rational, political motives for their collecting.[19] They ranged from royalist political sympathies and dreams to Jewish attempts to use collecting as a means to achieve, and publicly manifest, their assimilation into the Third Republic.

These are both fascinating, and thought-provoking books. McAuley raises an issue that is directly connected to Rococo collecting. He shows convincingly how

18 Caroline van Eck, *Piranesi's Candelabra and the Presence of the Past. Excessive Objects and the Emergence of a Style in the Age of Neoclassicism* (Oxford and New York: Oxford University Press, 2023).

19 James McAuley, *The House of Fragile Things. Jewish Art Collectors and the Fall of France* (New Haven and New York: 2021).

the inter-related Jewish families of the Reinach, Nissim de Camondo, and Ephrussi collected French eighteenth-century art, particularly of the reign of Louis XVI. Sometimes, as in the case of Moïse Nissim de Camondo, this had roots in a particular emotional investment to compensate somehow for the failure of his mariage and loss of his son. Above all, however, these families considered their collections as a way of connecting materially with France, its history and enlightenment ideals. But McAuley's book has a strange absence in its core: it does not really differentiate between the various styles of the period 1750-1800 collected: neo-classicism is its focus, but Camondo also avidly collected, and spent enormous sums on Rococo furniture, tapestry, paintings, and china [Figure 2.2].[20]

Now this is not simply an art historical quibble. Deciding to collect Rococo art and interior design is a highly connotated, if not debatable and loaded choice, and has been so since the style began to emerge in the 1710s. It is a style that moves entirely outside the parameters of classicism as defended by the Académie: no mythology, no imitation of classical subjects or figures or artists, no clear iconography, no following of the art of the *Grand Siècle* as embodied by Poussin; new genres, such as the *fête galante* introduced by Watteau; an art of the interior, and an art of women, commissioned and collected by female patrons. Not surprisingly, it has been criticized from its inception by critics and writers associated with official art politics and the Académie, with accusations ranging from the completely irrational to inciting to narcissism, because Rococo interiors replace allegorical or mythological painting by mirrors that endlessly reflect the image of the inhabitants of these spaces.[21] The Rococo, unlike Louis XVI neo-classicism, was certainly not considered by mainstream critics and art historians as the epitome of French art, the essence of French culture that the Jewish collectors in McAuley's book sought to integrate. Now there are a few plausible explanations for their preference: the Rococo is completely profane for instance, and in no way connected to Christianity, but this is clearly not the entire story.

In the context of this volume I do not want to delve deeper into the reasons for this preference for the Rococo of the Nissim de Camondo, Rothschilds, or Ephrussi and their relatives. What I do want to signal is that all approaches to collecting mentioned

20 This tendency to heap all eighteenth-century French art under the label of neoclassicism is even stronger in another recent study of Jewish collectors, Charles Dellheim's *Belonging and Betrayal. How Jews Made the Art World Modern* (Waltham: Brandeis University Press, 2021), who consistently calls the architect Germain Boffrand, one of the creators of the Rococo interior, a classicist architect; and the painter Greuze, the panter of bourgeois drama, a neo-classicist, thus suggesting he does not distinguish him from Jacques-Louis David, who was a neo-classical artist.

21 Partly these criticisms were part of the much older tradition, going back to Vitruvius, of rejecting all styles that did not adhere to classical ideals of proportion, harmony and rationality, as Ernst Gombrich has shown in his article on style in D.L. Stills (ed.), *International Encyclopedia of the Social Sciences* (New York, 1992). There was also a strong political subtext, with the style of the *Grand Siècle* propagated from the 1750s by art officials; but there was also a strong gender bias. See for instance Katie Scott, *The Rococo Interior: Decoration and Social Spaces in Early Eighteenth-Century Paris* (New Haven; London: Yale University Press, 1995), 81-241.

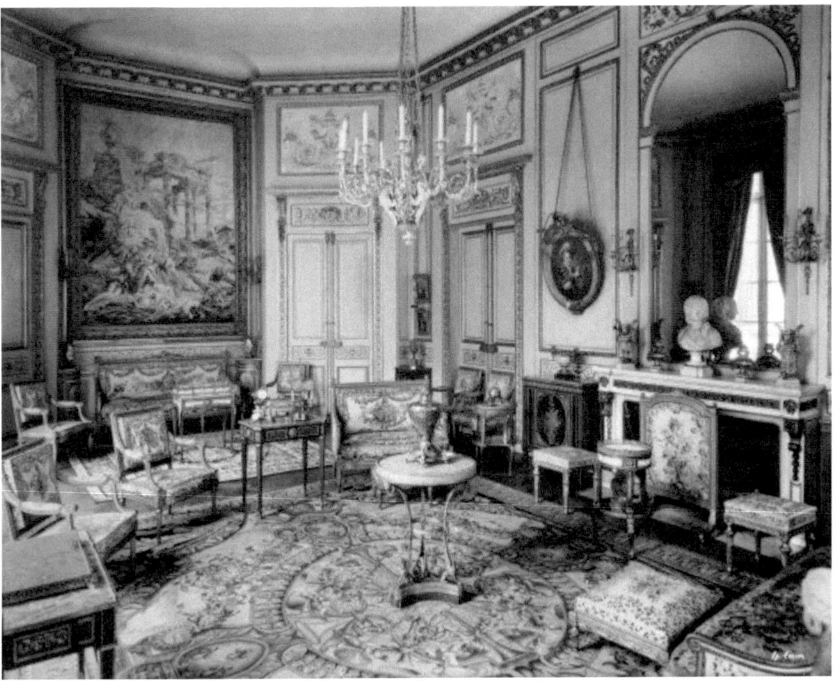

Figure 2.2: René Sergent (1865-1927), Hôtel Nissim de Camondo, Paris, 1911-14, view of the grand salon in 1936 (photo: Musée des Arts Décoratifs, Paris).

here, from psychoanalysis to the political histories recently evolved, suffer from a lack of fine-grained analysis of the individual features, the styles, and the materiality of the works collected, and what they tell us about their collecting. A case in point is the decision of the Jewish dealer and collector Nathan Wildenstein in 1905 to acquire the hôtel particulier that the architect Charles de Wailly, who designed the Théâtre de l'Odéon but who was also a master of the illusionistic interior filled with mirrors, had built for himself in the rue de la Boétie in Paris, to house his family, his collection and his shop. It still had its original wooden panelling, statues by Augustin Pajou and others, and cries out for a detailed analysis of the cultural meanings and affective materialities it carried for Wildenstein [Figure 2.3].[22]

This is not a minor issue, or simply an arthistorical hobby, particularly not in the light of the tension between intrinsic values and object attachments or investments mentioned earlier. In the rest of this paper I will therefore consider the Rococo in more detail, and

22 Dellheim, *Belonging and Betrayal*, 36-40, based on Jacques Hillairet, *Dictionnaire historique des rues de Paris* (Paris: Les Editions de Minuit, 1963), vol. II, 7-8; Alfred Fierro, *Histoire et Dictionnaire de Paris* (Paris: Robert Laffont, 2001), n.p. Intriguingly the Hôtel de Wailly was remodelled for Wildenstein by Walter-André Destailleur, the architect of Ferdinand de Rothschild's Waddesdon Manor.

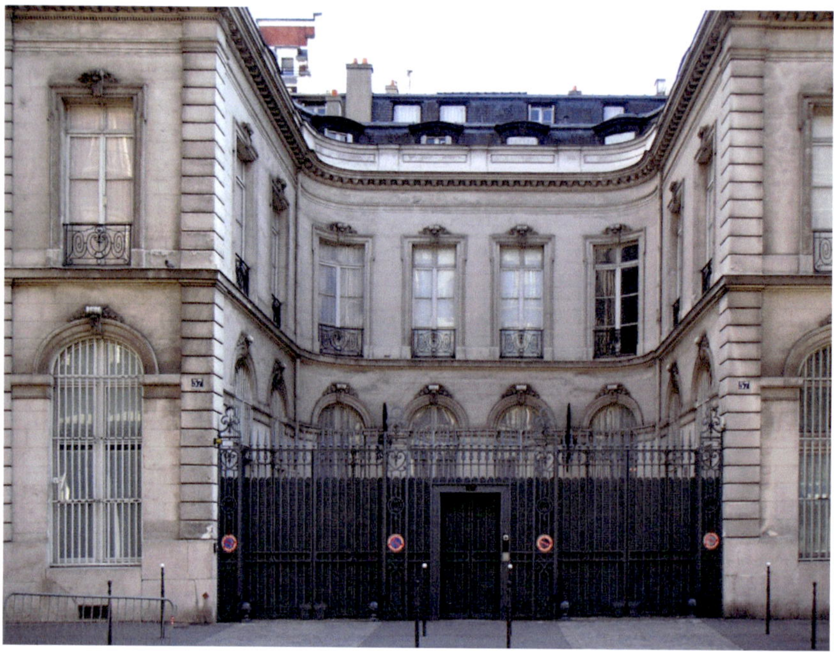

Figure 2.3: Charles de Wailly (1730-98), Hôtel de Wailly, now Institut Wildenstein, 1776, Paris: 57, rue de la Boétie (photo: Wikimedia Commons).

its history of collecting, from the start of the style in the work of Watteau to its collecting by the Goncourt brothers and others in the nineteenth century. It is not even work in progress, but rather a proposal for further research, but I do believe it may help advance our knowledge of the psychology of collecting, because a very similar set of works was collected by very different collectors, in very different periods and circumstances. At the very least it may help to re-assess some commonly held convictions about collectors and their motivations, such as the idea that collecting is a social elevator; or the sense of childhood loss and deprivation as a prime motivation for collecting.[23]

The aims of collecting

But before we do so, I want to distinguish a few varieties of collecting, not in the last place because I believe it won't bring us much to ask specifically what it is in Chinese

23 Gersaint for instance discusses the importance of collecting as a way of entry into higher echelons of society, but the architecture and art critic Marc-Antoine Laugier, best-known for his radical rejection of baroque and Rococo excess in architecture, was very critical of the social agendas underlying collecting. Cf Patrick Michel, *Peinture et plaisir: les goûts picturaux des collectionneurs parisiens au XVIIIe siècle* (Rennes: Presses Universitaires de Rennes, 2010), 383-5, and Stammers, *The Purchase of the Past*, 35.

porcelain that makes collector X collect it, or Dutch landscapes for collector Z; often it is more illuminating to ask for the purposes and aims of their collecting. Roughly I believe we can distinguish six large varieties

1. The collection as a display of trophies
2. The collection as the fulfillment of a particular taste, scientific interest or aesthetic preference.
3. The collection as a laboratory for art history: as the place where attributions are argued, hands recognized, oeuvre lists constituted, patterns of influence and schools established, and fakes distinguished from genuine works.
4. The collection as a memorial: what we might call the reliquary model, much used by Krysztof Pomian in France or Arthur McGregor in Britain as a major source for Western collecting and display; and also the starting-point for one of the first essays in the psychology of collecting, Goethe's novella *Der Sammler und die Seinigen* (1798), which gives a very full catalogue of object-investment in images, from portraits of ancestors, to locks of hair of dead loved ones; and a parade of responses by collectors, from disinterested aesthetic enjoyment to acute fetishism.[24]
5. The collection as a constituent of family or national heritage, an object of transmission and inheritance across families and generations.
6. And finally the collection as a fetish, a magical protection against the dangers of life, fear, unwanted desires etc.

These varieties can mix and mingle, most famously in the combination of the trophy, the inheritance, the national heritage, the memorial and the reliquary, a potent mix which until this very day explains many of the problems museums face when dealing with issues of ownership and restitution. Also, even in the most staid and demure scientific collection the collecting urge or frenzy, what the Dutch call *verzameldrift* and *verzamelwoede*, is rarely absent. But this still needs to be distinguished from what psychologists call hoarding, a pathological inability to throw anything away, close to a psychotic disorder, often caused by a deep fear or insecurity.

Collecting the Rococo in Paris 1715-40

The first case I want to discuss is that of two collectors of Watteau and other Rococo artists, Pierre Crozat (1665-1740) and Jeanne-Baptiste d'Albert de Luynes, Comtesse de Verrue (1670-1736). My discussion here is much indebted to Rochelle Ziskin's excellent *Sheltering Art. Collecting and Social Identity in Early Eighteenth-Century*

24 Pomian, Pomian, *Le musée, une histoire mondiale*, vol. 1, 114 - 154 and 345-92; Arthur MacGregor, *Curiosity and Enlightenment: Collectors and Collections from the Sixteenth to the Nineteenth Century* (New Haven and London: Yale University Press, 2007)

Paris.[25] Not only did they come from very different backgrounds, they also collected the same artists with very different aims, agendas, and from very different artistic or aesthetic convictions. Crozat was the son of a Toulouse banker. Together with his brother Antoine they became exceptionally rich financiers, with Antoine at some point buying the French American colonies from the Crown. Pierre, nicknamed 'le pauvre' also acted in court finance, but became more and more involved in art collecting, for himself, but also as the agent for the French Crown to negotiate the purchase of the collection of Queen Christina of Sweden, the major collection to appear on the market in the seventeenth century, which included large parts of the collection of the Habsburg Emperor Rudolf II. He had a townhouse built to the north of the Palais-Royal, in the area where bankers and collectors at the time flocked together; the Palais-Royal was the residence of the family of the King's brother, the Duc d'Orléans, and was home to the biggest art collection in France after the King's, with its conspicuous focus on Northern and Venetian art.

The Comtesse de Verrue descended from some of the most prominent French ducal famillies, and was close to the Rohan, who would transform the mediaeval hôtel de Guise in the Marais into the hôtel de Soubise, the first full statement of Rococo interior design created by Germain Boffrand. Verrue was married young to a Piemontese nobleman whom she disliked, subsequently became the mistress of the ruler of Savoye in Turin, and managed to escape to Paris in 1700. Much misrepresented through Alexandre Dumas' novel *Une femme de volupté*, she was in fact one of the major, original and most important collectors in France in the eighteenth century, with a collection that included nine to eleven Claudes, three to five Watteaus, two paintings by Rubens, various Wouwermans, Rembrandts and Van Dycks, and four Paters; as well as endless amounts of tropical birds, chandeliers, tapestries, and chinese porcelain. Her townhouse was located in the Faubourg Saint-Germain, near the rue du Cherche-Midi, and included Rococo ceilings by Audran, and a substantial library with one of the largest collections of female authors at the time.

We will come to the nature and differences in their collecting, but it should be noted first that both Crozat and Verrue's collecting activities were shaped by the particular political and artistic climate of the last years of the rule of Louis XIV. The kingdom suffered a sharp decline in political fortune, lost wars, and as a result the state withdrew from supporting the arts. Louis XIV died without an adult heir, but had appointed Philippe II d'Orléans as Regent. During the Regency the aristocracy moved from Versailles to Paris, which spurred a substantial wave of new building of townhouses in the Faubourg Saint-Germain on the left bank and new varieties of patronage that supported the new art of the Rococo. It was a period of speculative financial and colonial ventures; and the rise of the new aesthetic theories of Roger

---

25 Rochelle Ziskin, *Sheltering Art. Collecting and Social Identity in Early Eighteenth-Century Paris* (University Park: Pennsylvania State University Press, 2012).

de Piles and the Abbé du Bos, who stressed the immediate, pictorial effect of a work of art on the viewer and the *je ne sais quoi* as a feature of the art of painters such as Rubens or Titian, and Watteau, who worked in styles outside the theoretical precepts of the increasingly irrelevant Académie Royale de Penture. It was also the time of the second stage of the *Querelle des anciens et des modernes*, in which the role of women in cultural and intellectual life became a central issue.

Now what united these two collectors is their interest in, and patronage of the artist who embodied all that defined this new age of the Régence and the emerging Rococo: Antoine Watteau (1684-1721). By training and painting style originally a follower of Rubens, he invented a new genre, the *fête galante*, kept clear of the usual mythological or history paintings required by the Académy, and created an oeuvre that was intensely modern in the sense that it moved completely beyond, or besides, the classical tradition of the Grand Siècle. One of his most famous paintings, the *Enseigne de Gersaint* (1720-21), a shopsign he painted for one of his friends and patrons, the dealer in luxury goods Gersaint, summarizes his art as well as the Regency: it is a *fête galante* disguised as a shopsign, shows Louis XIV being packed off, and the modern art-loving middle classes entering the stage to buy and collect [Figure 2.4]. He stayed for a year in Crozat's house, in 1717, where he painted *L'embarquement pour Cythère*, which would give him admission to the Académie, and used Crozat's vast collection of Italian drawings as a laboratory of study. Verrue possessed at least three of his paintings, as well as the *Fête Champêtre* at the time attributed to Rubens, and now in Dresden, which was a major inspiration for Watteau's new genre [Figure 2.5]. She was also the central figure in a group of collectors which included the major collectors of Watteau's work, Jean de Jullienne, who was instrumental in creating his reputation by producing a collection of engravings after his work, and writing one of his first biographies and catalogue of works.

But their visions of their collection, their aims and ambitions were very different. Crozat collected very widely, but mainly the work of established Masters, and like the Duc d'Orléans, had a clear, and at the time new, preference for Venetian painting, Rubens and some Northern painters. After his journey to Italy in 1714-15 his collecting changed in nature, when with the help of Pierre-Jean Mariette, one of the fathers of connoisseurship, he transformed his collection into a laboratory for identifying hands and artists, detecting fakes, and producing rational arguments for attributions. Next to this on site activity the publication of his collection in the *Recueil Crozat*, one of the first catalogues in the modern sense, revolutionized the dissemination and thereby the accessability of collections.[26]

---

26 On Mariette see Smentek, *Mariette and the Science of the Connoisseur*; and Valérie Kobi, *Dans l'oeil du connaisseur: Pierre-Jean Mariette (1694-1774) et la construction des savoirs en histoire de l'art* (Rennes: Presses Universitaires de Rennes, 2017).

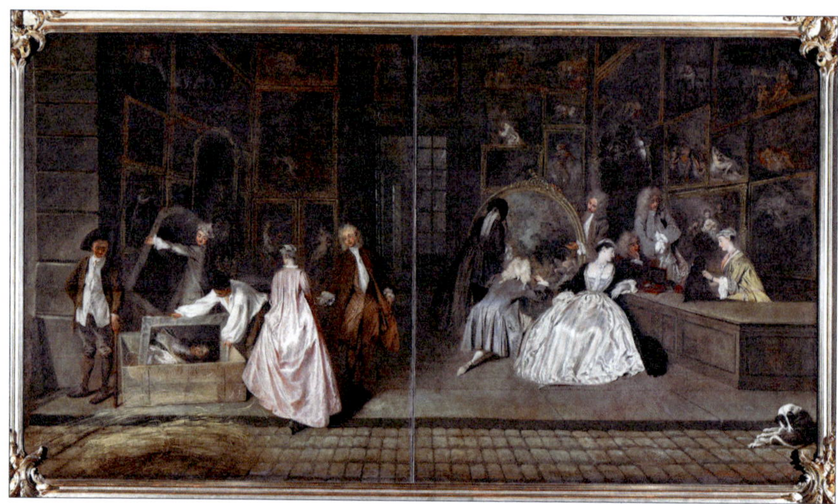

Figure 2.4: Antoine Watteau (1684-1721), Enseigne de Gersaint, 1720, oil on canvas, 163 x 306 cm, Berlin: Charlottenburg (photo: Wikimedia Commons).

Verrue, on the other hand, moved in the centre of royal power through her close relation to the Duc de Bourgogne, for a long time third in line for the succession to Louis XIV. She was also a central figure in the circle of Modern intellectuals; her artistic preferences move completely outside the accepted preferences of either the Académie, the Duc d'Orléans or even Crozat, as she was one of the first to collect consistently Dutch masters such as Wouwerman, Mieris or Adriaen van de Velde before that fashion really started in the 1750s.[27] She collected Watteau and his followers, but also the major Flemish painters Van Dyck and Rubens. But the purpose of this collecting was not to create a laboratory for visual art history and the science of attribution; nor to publish the collection in sets of reproductive engravings. Instead, it served, first of all, the aesthetic delectation of the Comtesse and her large circle of friends, family and servants. Next, through a culture of gifts and testaments, it served to construct, uphold and cement a close-knit circle of friends and family members who shared political, artistic and social ideas; an aristocratic, closed society in short, but at the same time with very modern ideas. Or, as Ziskin puts it, a culture of collecting and particularly gifting distinguished by 'elite inclusion and disdain of monetary value'.[28]

So if we want to define the collecting of Crozat and Verrue in terms of the three main terms used in this context in the 18th century -- *amateur*, *curieux* and *connoisseur*, with the *curieux* defined by a great desire to learn and invest in seeing and possessing new, rare and exceptional things in the *Dictionnaire* of the Académie française of 1694

27 Patrick Michel, *Peinture et plaisir*, 177-222.

28 Ziskin, *Sheltering Art*, p. 207.

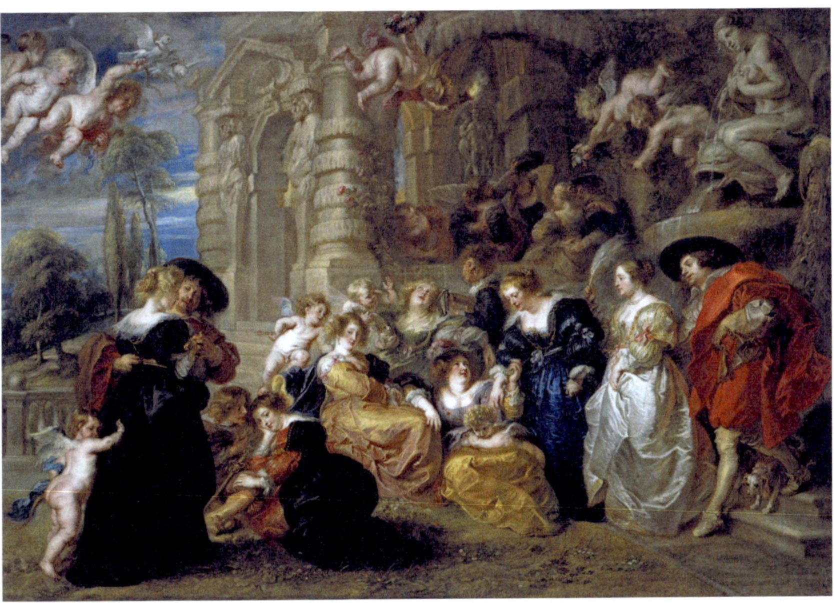

Figure 2.5: Peter Paul Rubens (1577-1640), The Garden of Love [previously called Fête Champêtre], 1630-31, oil on canvas, 199 x x286 cm, Madrid: Prado (photo: Wikimedia Commons).

-- it is clear that Crozat fits very well into all three categories; but for Verrue the case is not so clear, not in the last place because all these terms refer exclusively to men. She was definitely an *amateur* and a *curieuse*, and probably a *connoisseur* as well, but one who refused to subscribe to the codification of connoisseurship and its relations to the art market that was developed in Crozat's collection.

Verrue's collection and collecting pattern would have a long afterlife, as it soon became a symbol, for the critics of Rococo such as Louis Petit de Bachaumont, Etienne La Font de Saint-Yenne and Jean-Jacques Rousseau for a female, effeminate and superficial style of art and life; whereas the Masters increasingly favoured by Crozat as he grew older stood for a masculine, sober, classical and noble simplicity. One can see where this would lead to all kinds of implications for the politics of taste: in the public and private faces of Mme de Pompadour's collecting and patronage, for instance, who preferred Boucher when at home, but publicly sponsored a return to the style of the *Grand Siècle*, as part of a public campaign of state sponsorship of the arts that would restore the monarchy to its seventeenth-century glory and at the same time gloss over her bourgeois antecedents.[29] The same combination of artistic

29 Richard Wittman, *Architecture, Print Culture, and the Public Sphere in Eighteenth-Century France* (New York: Routledge, 2007), 97-114.

and sexual politics was played out in the public perception of Marie-Antoinette's patronage of Rococo art.

At the same time, these three categories of the *amateur*, the *connoisseur* and the *curieux* also serve as important pointers to the kind of psychology associated with collecting. We do find the notion of the interest in things, characteristic of the amateur; but all three concepts have a very strong epistemological, empirical bias, and very little space for the affects, emotions or psychological needs that may drive collecting: they are all about interest in the empirical world, curiosity, acquiring visual knowledge, and the ability to make use of visual perception to understand artefacts.

Rococo collecting in the nineteenth century

Now if we jump a century, the revival of interest in the Rococo in France is generally attributed to the collecting and publications of Edmond and Jules de Goncourt: their jointly-written books *L'art du XVIIIe siècle* and *La femme au XVIIIe siècle*, with its portraits of major figures such as Mme de Pompadour or Marie-Antoinette gave words to, and legitimized, the enjoyment of Rococo art which in fact had started as early as the Empire. As the literary historian Simches already showed in 1964, the Rococo had never stopped, except for a brief interlude during the early days of the French Revolution, to attract and fascinate not only collectors, but the public as well.[30] The important role of the poets Gérard de Nerval and Théophile Gautier is well known. They set up house in 1834 in the impasse du Doyenné (now demolished), a part of the former hôtel de Rambouillet, near the Louvre, a dilapidated street which housed an immense salon of the eighteenth century with its boiseries and mouldings intact. Here they collected work by Fragonard and Boucher bought for next to nothing, and organized parties in which they produced pastiches after Watteau and others.[31] Balzac describes this street in his two great novels of human-thing entanglement, collecting, and using Rococo objects to manipulate humans, *La Cousine Bette* and *Le Cousin* Pons. There is thus a direct connection between the generation of 1830 and the Goncourts, because, as Marc Fumaroli has recently shown, the Goncourts were much inspired by the presence of the eighteenth century in the *Comédie humaine*. *Le Cousin Pons* collects its paintings and objects; he gives a fan painted by Watteau and possessed by Mme de Pompadour to his niece, who doesn't recognize its worth, to name but one of the endless manifestations of the eighteenth-century palimpsest in the *Comédie Humaine*. Inspired by Balzac the Goncourts wanted to

30 Seymour Simches, *Le romantisme et le goût esthétique du XVIIIe siècle* (Paris: Presses Universitaires de France, 1964); see also Carol Duncan, *The Pursuit of Pleasure. The Rococo Revival in French Romantic Art* (New York: Garland, 1976).

31 Gérard de Nerval, 'La Rue du Doyenné', in *Petits châteaux en Bohème* (1853) (Paris: Classiques Garnier, 1958), 8-11. On Nerval's interest in the Rococo see Ken Ireland, *Cythera Regained: The Rococo Revivsl in European Literature and the Arts 1830-1910* (Madison: Fairleigh Dickinson University Press, 2006); Allison Unruh, *Aspiring to La Vie Galante: Reincarnations of Rococo in the Second Empire* (PhD thesis New York University, 2008).

do the same for that century, but lacked Balzac's literary talent and ability to convey this historical layeredness. But there is this long presence, or persistence, of the fascination with the Rococo before and after the Goncourt brothers.[32]

At the same time, the articulacy and renown of the Goncourt work has obscured the fact that, while this taste for the Rococo was there, there also was much resistance in France to considering the Rococo, as the Goncourts did, as the epitome of French taste and artistic grandeur. There may have been a strong fashion for the eighteenth century from the 1860s onwards, which percolated from the court into the bourgeoisie, nourished by the Empress Eugénie's attempts to model herself on Marie-Antoinette. Eugénie for instance organized an exhibition about Marie-Antoinette in the Petit Trianon in 1867, for which the collector Léopold Double, one of the first nineteenth-century collectors of Rococo art on a major scale, loaned many pieces. Subsequently, many of his art works were acquired by Moïse Nissim de Camondo, which shows something of the complex trajectory of such artefacts.[33] It was always obvious, however, and particularly manifest in state patronage, that the style of the Grand Siècle of Louis XIV would be the most apt expression of French identity, and not the *style rocaille*.[34] This use of the *Grand Siècle* coalesced for instance around the conservation of Versailles, and Louis-Philippe's decision to turn part of that palace into a national museum of French history.

Conclusion

This brief excursion into eighteenth-century collecting of what was at the time contemporary art shows, I hope, that for collectors such as Crozat or Verrue the emotional entanglement with a collection that became such a feature of subsequent, often fictional accounts of collectors, does not seem to have played an important role. Even when we take into account that surviving accounts of collecting such as the prefaces by Gersaint are not ego documents that would tell something about emotional involvements, it seems clear their collecting should be understood in terms of sociability, curiosity, connoisseurship, and more generally as part of the eighteenth-century interest in developing visual rather than textual varieties of knowledge. Nor was the Rococo the obvious choice for a Jewish collector like Moïse Nissim de Camondo that McAuley, Stammers and other historians of collecting make it out to be. Even apart from their lack of distinguishing Rococo from neo-classicism, or the patronage of Mme de Pompadour from that of Marie-Antoinette, McAuley's

32 Marc Fumaroli, "Le 'siècle' des Goncourts ou le XVIIIe siècle réhabilité," in Jean-Louis Cabanès a.o. (eds.), *Les Goncourts dans leur siècle - Un siècle de Goncourts* (Villeneuve d'Asq: Les Presses du Septentrion, 2020), 17-30. See also Katie Scott and Melissa Hyde (eds.), *Rococo Echo: Art, History and Historiography from Cochin to Coppola* (Oxford: Voltaire Foundation, 2014).

33 Cf Stammers, *The Purchase of the Past*,225-28.

34 On Eugénie and Marie-Antoinette see Stammers, *The Purchase of the Past*, 215 ff., particularly on the exhibition Eugénie patronized at the Petit Trianon about Marie-Antoinette.

account, like that of Pierre Assouline, the most recent French biographer of Camondo for that matter, raises more questions than it answers. Why these preferences? Were they simply driven by peer pressure, or by a rather vague idea that the late eighteenth century embodied the essence of Frenchness? But then what about Marie-Antoinette, a foreigner like the Jewish collectors, whose assimilation, like theirs, was in the end less than successful? Was this really all about creating the illusion of complete order, imitating the order and dominance of nature of the court of Louis XIV? And if Louis XIV was a hidden model, how does this relate to the actual appearance -- asymmetrical, frivolous, feminine, apolitical -- of the pieces Camondo collected?[35]

This needs much more work and archival digging. At the same time, it is clear that as Camondo grew older, the provenance of his pieces became more important, culminating in the acquisition of two vases he believed had been touched by Marie-Antoinette herself. We have clearly moved here into the atmosphere of the collection as a reliquary, analysed by Goethe in *Der Sammler und die Seinigen*.

But apart from all these historical questions, I believe that this exercise also raises a wider issue: that of the position of the history of collecting as a discipline. It is clear, I hope to have shown, that McAuley's account is very successful in its ambition to place Camondo's collecting of eighteenth-century art into a variety of collecting behaviour that had very wide personal and political resonances, which moved it far beyond the narrow confines of buying and displaying art. But that at the same time, many of the questions it raises spring from a lack of arthistorical awareness. Ultimately the tension between intrinsic value attributed to objects and their roles as elements in a collection remains unaddressed.

These complex relations as they are raised in the evolution of the history of collecting from an ancillary discipline to art history, to its recent flowering as an independent branch of history reflects, in my view, the recent shift power balance in the relations between academic and museum research in art history, where it are now increasingly the museums who have the time and manpower to do research, but with very different agendas and contraints than departments of art history.

35 McAuley, *The House of Fragile Things*, 120-26.

From Hegel to Freud

Imperial Museums and the Rise of Psychology in the History of Culture, between Triumphalism and Criticism

Pascal Griener, École du Louvre, Paris

Introduction

Vienna's 'fin de siècle' was the *locus* where collecting and psychology became entwined for good. Freud, who lived in Vienna most of his life (his address was Berggasse 19), was not only the founder of psychoanalysis, but also an avid collector of archaeological artefacts. By 1908, he occupied the entire first floor of the building. His family quarters were situated on the left-hand side of the landing. He installed his own 'cabinet' on the right-hand side of the same landing: a waiting room, his consultation room, and his own office [Figure 3.1]. These three spaces were crammed with archaeological objects and with framed prints. Several patients commented upon the fact that they felt that they did not enter a consultation room, but rather a museum.[1] Freud expressed himself very rarely on his own practice as a collector. Yet Archaeology played a major role in his theoretical writings, as a pervading model. Freud describes psychoanalysis as a kind of archaeology; its aim is to uncover deeply

---

1 On Freud's collection, the following publications stand out for their quality: Eds. Lynn Gamwell, Richard Wells, Intr. Peter Gay, *Sigmund Freud and Art. His Personal Collection of Antiquities* (London: Thames & Hudson, New York: State University of New York, 1989); Lynn Gamwell, Richard Wells, eds., *The Sigmund Freud Antiquities. Fragments from a buried past* (Boston: Boston University Art Gallery, 1992); Stephen Barker ed., *Excavations and their objects. Freud's collection of Antiquity* (New York: State University of New York Press, 1996).

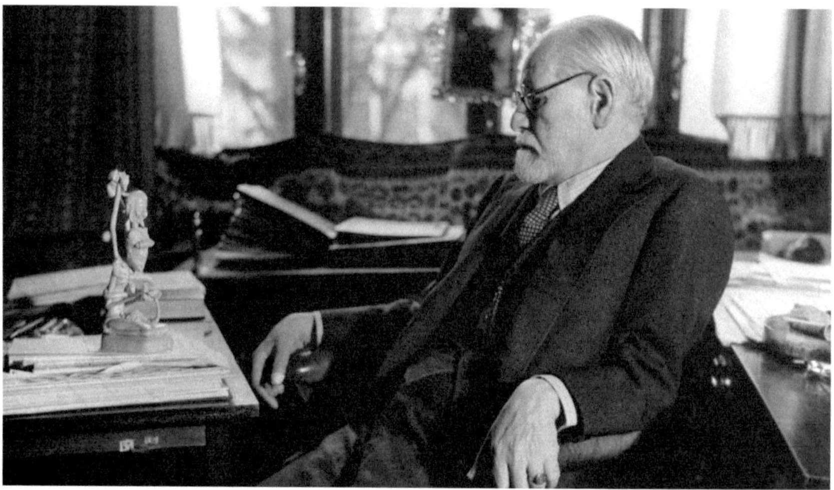

Figure 3.1: Sigmund Freud at his desk, Berggasse 19, Vienna. 1937.

unknown remains, accumulating in layers within the depths of the human psyche. This 'mental archaeology' was first applied to individuals; Freud delved into the unconscious segments of his patients' mind. He published very few texts related to the psychological dimension of collecting; but in 1908, he published "Character and Anal Erotism", a study on the basic human need for possession and its deep psychic implications.[2] One year later, he devoted an entire conference to the notion of fetishism.[3] But Freud had a further ambition: to extend the validity of his methods to the long-tern development of the Human psyche in History, and to study the fate of entire civilizations.[4] Such an idea was not new at the time. From Wilhelm Wundt to Ernst von Brücke, from Richard Semon to Aby Warburg and to Heinrich Wölfflin, most German scientists believed that psychology had become a field of first importance, because it was hoped that it could provide a key to the understanding of the human mind, be it in its conscious or unconscious components.[5] The purpose of psychology was to explain the laws that regulated the human psyche in the course of history, even if individuals were never aware of these rules and of their mutations. Charles Darwin, the most famous scientist of his age, had designed an overarching

2 Sigmund Freud, "Charakter und Analerotik," in *Gesammelte Werke*, VII (Frankfurt: Fischer, 1999), 203-209.

3 Hans Lobner and Louis Rose, "'Zur Genese des Fetischismus'. Ein Wiederentdeckter Vortrag Sigmund Freuds," *Sigmund Freud House Bulletin* 14, no.1, (1990), 3-20; Hartmut Böhme, "Fetishismus und Sexualität. Auf den Weg zu einen metapsychologischen Konzept. Binet, Krafft-Ebing, Freud," in *Kulturtheorie*, ed. Ortrud Gutjahr (Würzburg: Köningshausen & Neumann, 2005), 161-184.

4 Michel de Certeau, "Ce que Freud fait de l'histoire," *Annales ESC* (May, June 1970), 654-667.

5 Louis Rose, *The Freudian calling. Early Viennese Psychoanalysis and the pursuit of cultural science* (Detroit: Wayne State University Press, 1998).

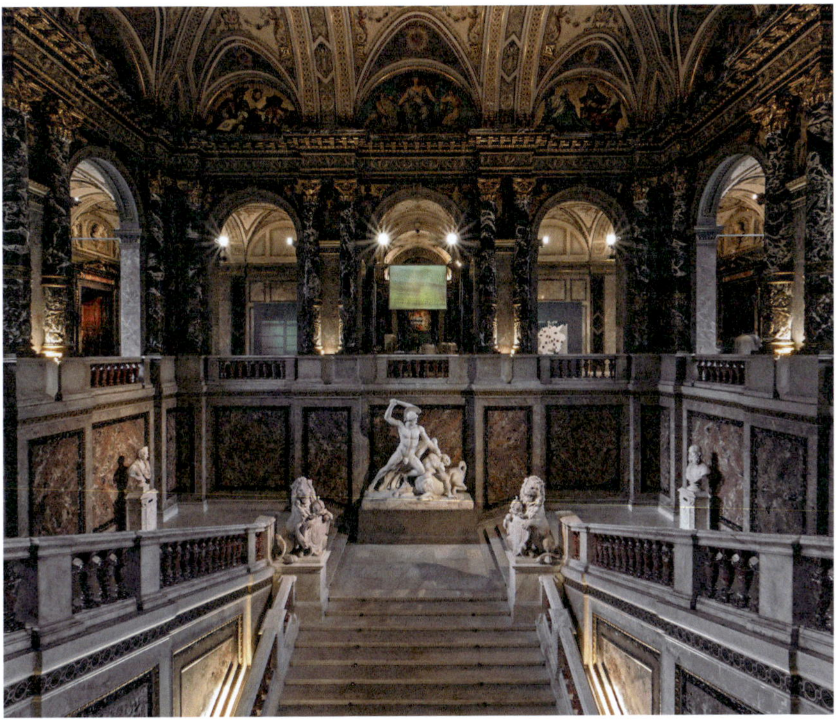

Figure 3.2: Great Staircase, Kunsthistorisches Museum, Vienna, adorned according to a program by Albert Ilg. On the landing, Antonio Canova's sculpture, *Theseus and the Centaur.*1804-1819. Marble.

model in order to explain how species evolved through selection and adaptation in the course of thousands of years, according to precise laws and patterns, and how these transformations were inherited genetically. This ambitious model was much admired, and its architecture inspired many scientists. Freud thought that he could reap much benefit from a historical study spanning entire civilizations.

Freud discovered his ambition as a philosopher of culture in Vienna, as a direct response to his museum environment and to his own collection of archaeological artefacts. Collecting and contemplating objects in a museum environment is an intellectual pursuit, which has the same impact as the reading of theoretical texts. The Imperial museums in Vienna could boast of vast holdings, documenting almost all known civilizations [Figure 3.2]. The opening of the Kunsthistorisches Museum and of the Naturhistorisches Museum vastly increased the fame of the imperial collections, which were generously open to the public. Freud frequented the KHM with assiduity. His own collection betrays his wish to possess his own little museum, full of authentic archaeological finds. But Freud's collection had a highly personal dimension. As a Jew himself, he was passionate about the history of the Jewish people. Their past existence is documented by several ancient texts, but unlike the Greeks, the Romans or the Egyptians, the Jews from the Old Testament had left remarkably little material archaeological evidence. Freud's father owned Ludwig Philippson's *Die Israelitische Bibel* (1839-54), a famous and popular Bible at the time in the German world. This edition compensated for the lack of material evidence for ancient Jewish culture: the text of the Old Testament was lavishly illustrated with *Egyptian* scenes and objects drawn from ancient Egyptian monuments. Thanks to what can be described as a substitution, the history of the Elected People could be evidenced, albeit through a material culture belonging to those who kept the Jews under their yoke for several centuries. Philippson 's choice was not totally indefensible, inasmuch as the Old Testament shows that the biblical history of the Jews is entwined with that of Pharaonic Egypt.[6] For Freud, the problem was even more simple: Moses himself was, by birth, an Aegyptian prince.

In effect, *Der Mann Moses* (1939) – Freud's last book, which was written in the most dramatic circumstances, Austria's annexation by the German Reich and the triumph of Nazism - took a radical stance against the ideologies which were crafted in the age of imperial museums during the nineteenth century.[7] These ideologies drew massively upon Hegel's philosophy of History.

Psychology as a dominant science in the XIXth century

At the end of the nineteenth century, the German states could boast that they had the best scientists in the field of psychology – especially the Austro-Hungarian empire, Saxony and the Prussian state. The German-speaking contribution to psychology followed two directions. First, it led to the development of experimental psychology. A German professor from Dresden, Georg Theodor Fechner, explained perceptions with the help of the laws of physics, duly evidenced by experiments and measures.[8] He enjoyed a high reputation in the art world, because in 1871 he had managed to prove beyond any doubt, both through a historical and an optic investigation, that the *Dresden Madonna* by Hans Holbein the younger, was not

6 Jan Assmann, *Moses der Ägypter* (Munich: Hanser, 2001); Guy Stroumsa, *Religions d'Abraham. Histoires croisées* (Genève: Labor et Fides, 2017); Pascal Griener, "The Fascination for Egypt During the Eighteenth Century. History of a 'Configuration,'" in *Beyond Egyptomania. Objects, Style and Agency*, ed. Miguel John Versluys (Berlin: de Gruyter, 2020), 53-70.

7 Sigmund Freud, *Der Mann Mose und die Monotheistische Religion. Drei Abhandlungen* (Amsterdam: Allert de Lange, 1939). On the imperial ideology in Europe at the time, Christoph Kampmann, Franz Bosbach, Hermann Hiery, eds., *Imperium / Empire / Reich, Ein Konzept politischer Herrschaft im deutsch-britischen Vergleich* (Munich: Saur, 1999).

8 Gustav Theodor Fechner, *Elemente der Psychophysik* (Leipzig: Breitkopf und Härtel, 1860); Ulla Fix, ed., *Fechner und die Folgen außerhalb der Naturwissenschaften: interdisziplinäres Kolloquium zum 200. Geburts-tag Gustav Theodor Fechners* (Tübingen : Niemeyer, 2003); Renée Bouveresse-Quilliot, *L'esthétique expérimentale* (Paris: Ellipses, 1999).

an original painting, but a 17th century copy after a painting by Holbein then in possession of the Hohenzollern family.[9] Another scientist, Ernst von Brücke, was professor at Vienna university.[10] A keen connoisseur of the imperial collections, he pointed out that through their very artistic practice, several old masters made very valuable contributions to visual psychology; for example, Brücke noticed that the depiction of light, in Francesco Furini's *Magdalen*, is totally wrong, but that the mind of the viewer instinctively reads this application of the chiaroscuro as a *coded sign*, as *the denotation* of a shadow. Furini's *Magdalen* is thus not at all a mere mimetic representation: empirically, the artist had guessed that his way of painting shadows would be processed by the mind of the viewers, who would interpret those as schemata, as signs of shadows. The implications of such an analysis for connoisseurship were of course very significant.

A second type of psychology that developed at the time was *collective psychology*. Specialists tried to produce a model of the collective psyche in history. One of the most productive minds in that field was Wilhelm Wundt, whose concept of "Völkerpsychologie" was first discussed in an essay published in 1863.[11] Wundt – whose writings fascinated Aby Warburg – had the ambition of becoming what Charles Darwin, with his *Origin of Species* (1859) was within the science of life: the revolutionary proponent of a theory outlining the evolution of the human psyche through its entire history. Within this history, physiological trends worked on the collective psyche of entire civilizations, unbeknown to the individuals involved. A given culture was to be defined, not only by its ideals, by its beliefs, but also by its physiological, its conscious or unconscious characteristics. Wundt was not satisfied with Fechner's experimental psychology, because it was too positivistic.[12]

Hegel, civilisations and universal museums

This foray of psychology into history was made possible by one single fact of huge importance: the rising impact of the philosophy of History propagated by Joseph Görres, Georg Wilhelm Hegel and the latter's disciples in the German-speaking world.

---

9 Gustav Theodor Fechner, *Ueber die Aechtheitsfrage der Holbein'schen Madonna. Discussion und Acten* (Leipzig: Breitkopf, Härtel, 1871).

10 Pascal Griener, "Connoisseurship et sciences cognitives: la leçon du XIXe siècle européen," in *Connoisseurship, l'oeil, la raison et l'instrument; actes du colloque École du Louvre en partenariat avec la Fondation Calouste Gulbenkian et l'Institut national d'histoire de l'art 20, 21 et 22 octobre 2011*, ed. Patrick Michel (Paris: École du Louvre, 2014), 291-305; Theodor von Frimmel, "Ernst Wilh. von Brücke in seinen Beziehungen zu Kunst und Kunstwissenschaft," *Kunstchronik*, N.F.3 (1892), 421-423.

11 Wilhelm Wundt, *Vorlesungen über die Menschen- und Thierseele.* vol. 1. [ed. W. Nitsche. Berlin: Deutscher Verlag der Wissenschaften, 1990, 2 vols] (Leipzig: Voss, 1863); Wilhelm Wundt, *Völkerpsychologie. Eine Untersuchung der Entwicklungsgesetze von Sprache, Mythus und Sitte. Band 1: Die Sprache. Teil 1 und 2* (Leipzig: Kröner, 1900); Berthold Oelze, *Wilhelm Wundt. Die Konzeption der Völkerpsychologie* (Münster: Waxmann, 1991).

12 Serge Nicolas, "Wundt et la fondation en 1879 de son laboratoire," *L'Année psychologique* 105, no.1 (January 2005), 133-170.

Johann Joseph Görres was an German intellectual who during the First Empire, dreamt of liberating the German people from Napoléon's yoke. Yet after the Restoration, he was appalled by the conservative policies embraced by the European sovereigns after the congress at Vienna (1815). He believed that within such a dramatic context, only the Roman Christian religion could lead the struggle for autonomy by the German people. Görres underlined the central role of Religion as a force that led civilisations to Progress and Emancipation. Görres thought that the most primitive religions in antiquity were enslaving the minds of worshippers; he compared their state to that of human beings unaware of the consequences of their own actions. However, in the course of History, Religion favoured the emancipation of the human spirit. This view is stated in Görres' *Wachstum der Historie* (1807).[13] His theory set out to prove that Religion was a forerunner of Philosophy, within a teleological vision of History.

Georg Wilhelm Friedrich Hegel made an extensive use of Görres's theory; he radicalized his own philosophy of history, which celebrated the slow but irreversible emancipation of the Spirit in Universal History. Art became a decisive, albeit intermediary moment within the development of the Spirit in History towards the age when Philosophy would ultimately take over from Religion. Such a philosophical construction bore consequences on Hegel' own representation of Art. He lectured on the subject, but his notes were published only after his death. From 1832 onwards, Hegel's students collected his *Nachlass*, and produced the first complete edition of Hegel's works.[14] In 1835, his lectures on Aesthetics were published by one of his disciples, Heinrich Gustav Hotho.[15] Hegel's vision of humanity, as determined by the development of the spirit of the world [Weltgeist] in history, was expanded in his lectures on the philosophy of history, which he delivered between 1822 and 1827. For Hegel, Art is a production of the mind, and as such, allows the historian to grasp the

---

13 Joseph Görres, *Wachstum der Historie*. In: *Geistesgeschichtliche und literarische Schriften* I (1803-1808). (=Joseph Görres. *Gesammelte Schriften*, vol.III), ed. Günther Müller (Cologne: Gilde, 1926), 363-440.

14 Georg Wilhelm Friedrich Hegel, *Werke. Vollständige Ausgabe durch einen Verein von Freunden des Verewigten*, 18 vols. (Berlin, 1832-1845); Jean-Louis Vieillard-Baron, *Hegel et l'idéalisme allemand* (Paris: Vrin, 1999), 223 et s.

15 Heinrich Gustav Hotho, ed., *Hegel, Vorlesungen über die Aesthetik* 3 vols. (Berlin, 1835). On Hegel and art history during the XIXth century, Dan Karlholm, "Reading the Virtual Museum of General Art History," *Art History* 24, no. 4 (September 2001), 552-577; Daniel Fulda, *Wissenschaft aus Kunst. Die Entstehung der modernen deutschen Geschichtsschreibung 1760-1860* (Berlin: de Gruyter, 1996); Otto Gerhard Oexle, "Die Geschichtswissenchaften im Zeichen des Historismus," *Historische Zeitschrift* 238 (1984), 17-55; Petra Kuhlmann-Hodick, Das *Kunstgeschichtsbild. Zur Darstellung von Kunstgeschichte und Kunsttheorie in der deutschen Kunst des 19. Jahrhunderts*, 2 vols (Bern: Lang, 1996); Monika Wagner. *Allegorie und Geschichte. Austattungsprogramme öffentlicher Gebäude des 19. Jahrhunderts in Deutschland* (Tübingen: Wasmuth, 1989); Annemarie Menke-Schwinghammer, *Weltgeschichte als 'Nationalepos': Wilhelm von Kaulbachs Kulturhistorischer Zyklus im Treppenhaus des Neuen Museums in Berlin*, (Berlin: Deutscher Verlag für Kunstwissenschaft, 1994).

development of the Human mind in History. Any art work requires a psychological approach, because it cast a light on the mind of the artist who, within the precise context of his civilization, produced an artefact.

Hegel's philosophy of History, seen as the History of the rise of the Spirit throughout the ages, had a tremendous impact in the world of museums, especially in the German world. In France, after the Revolution of 1848, the Hegelian model of the history of humanity was hailed as a perfect narrative in the highest circles of power. The government commissioned a series of paintings to Paul Chenavard, in order to adorn the former church Ste Geneviève, which the 1848 government wanted to turn again into a pantheon [Figure 3.3].[16] Chenavard, who was a philosophical mind and had met Hegel himself in Italy, sketched out a true Hegelian representation of history in its different stages. In Berlin, from 1845 to 1865, Wilhelm von Kaulbach embarked on a vast philosophical-historical cycle for the Neues Museum, based upon the ideas of Görres and of Hegel.[17] Even in Great Britain, Hegel's impact was being felt. In the museum world, his vision of history became known and highly fashionable after a British writer, George Henry Lewes, published a detailed account of Hegel' newly published *Aesthetik* in 1842.[18] This text in turn inspired a British artist, James Stephanoff, who created a museum display of ancient sculptures in his watercolour: *An Assemblage of Works of Art, from the Earliest Period to the Time of Phidias*. The work was exhibited in 1845 in London, and it convinced the sculptor Richard Westmacott that he should apply an Görrian and Hegelian program to the pediment of the British Museum (1846-52) [Figure 3.4].[19] This pediment expands the history of

---

16 Joseph Sloane, *Paul Marc Joseph Chenavard, artist of 1848* (Chapel Hill: University of North Carolina Press, 1962), chapter 5; Thomas Schiesser, *Paul Chenavard: monuments de l'échec, 1807-1895* (Paris: Presses du Réel, 2009), 26; Théophile Gautier (avec la collaboration de Gérard de Nerval), "Panthéon, peintures murales par Chenavard," *La Presse*, 5 au 11 septembre 1848, repris dans *L'Art moderne* (Paris: Levy, 1856), 1-94; Jean Richer, "La description du "Panthéon" de Paul Chenavard par Gautier et Nerval : une collaboration inconnue," *Archives des Lettres modernes* 48 (1963/2). Chenavard represented Napoleon I in the nave of history, drawing n°38 in Thomas Schlesser (ref above). In 1855, at the Universal exhibition, Chenavard's cartoons for the Pantheon were exhibited, like Wilhelm von Kaulbach's designs for the Munich Pinakothek. Chenavard's cartoons were exhibited once again in Brussels in 1864. Charles Blanc, *Exposition des cartons de Paul Chenavard pour la décoration du Panthéon* (Lyon, Palais Saint-Pierre. Paris: typogr. G. Chamerot, 1876).

17 Monika Wagner. *Allegorie und Geschichte. Austattungsprogramme öffentlicher Gebäude des 19. Jahrhunderts in Deutschland* (Tübingen: Wasmuth, 1989), 126 and s.

18 George Henry Lewes, "The philosophy of art: Hegel's Aesthetics," *British and Foreign Review* XIII, no. 25 (1842), 1-49. On several publications, but also on Hegel's *Vorlesungen über die Aesthetik*. (1835).

19 Westmacott provided a description of this pediment; it was published in *The British Museum, in five sections, or, how to view the whole at once* (Londres: Cradock, 1852), 7 and s., and in the *Illustrated London News*, May 29, 1852, together with a sketch of the art work itself; Ian Jenkins, "James Stephanoff and the British Museum," *Apollo* (March 1985), 174-181; Jonah Siegel, *Material Inspirations: The Interests of the Art Object in the Nineteenth Century and After* (Oxford: Oxford University Press, 2020).

humanity from its most primitive stages to the heights of the British Empire.[20] In his own explanation for the program, Westmacott say that "Commencing at the western end or angle of the pediment, Man is represented emerging from a rude savage stage through the influence of religion. (...) Paganism prevails, and becomes diffused by means of the Arts." At a later stage, which is depicted on the right-hand side of the pediment, Science takes over from religion to guide Man to Progress. When the pediment was inaugurated in 1852, Ferenc Pulszki wrote an essay where he sketched out in great detail the Hegelian model as an ideal that should be applied to great museums: "On the progress and decay of art; and on the rearrangement of a national museum".[21] Much later, the Kunsthistorisches Museum subscribed to the same idea, although this reference was made through other channels. The visitor crossing the threshold to the great staircase of the Kunsthistorisches Museum, was struck by a gigantic statue by Antonio Canova adorning the first landing: *Theseus and the Centaur*.[22] Theseus was considered to be the mythical founder of the Acropolis in Athens, and his name was believed to mean *institution* according to a well-known etymology at the time ("Thesmos").[23] Originally, this colossal sculpture had been commissioned for the Foro imperiale in Milan during the Napoleonic period. After 1815, the Habsburg family bought this piece of spolia, and in 1891, when it was exhibited in the grand staircase of the museum, it became an allegory of the triumph of the Habsburgs over Napoleon. Theseus's fight against the centaur symbolizes the struggle between civilization

---

20 On Hegel and the British intellectuals of the Nineteenth Century, see Stephan Houlgate, *An Introduction to Hegel* (Oxford: Blackwell, 2005), 16; Lucia Pradella, "Hegel, Imperialism and Universal History," *Science & Society* 78, no.4 (2014), 426-453; Giuseppe Micheli, Gregorio Piaia, Giovanni Santinello, eds., *Models of the History of Philosophy*: Volume IV: *The Hegelian Age*, (Cham: Springer, 2022), 580 et s; James Bradley, "Hegel in Britain. A brief history of British commentary and attitude," *Heythrop Journal* XX (1979), 1-24; Kirk Willis, "The introduction and critical reception of Hegelian thought in Britain 1830-1900", *Victorian studies* XXXII (1988-89), 85-111.

21 Gabor Ebli, *National Museums and civic patrons. Practices of cultural accumulation in central and eastern Europe* (Paris: Harmattan, 2020), 21 and s.; on Pulszki, Benedicte Savoy, Andrea Meyer, *The Museum is open. Towards a transnational history of museums 1750-1940* (Berlin: de Gruyter, 2014), 35 et s; Ferenc Pulszky, "On the progress and decay of art; and on the rearrangement of a national museum," in *The Museum of Classical Antiquities, A Quarterly Journal of Ancient Art*, II (March 1852), 1-15; see Ferenc Pulszky, *Meine Zeit, Mein Leben*, 4 vols. (Leipzig: Stämpfel, 1881-83). He knew the Habsburg collections very well, and published several essays on their content.

22 This sculpture was completed in November 1819 by Antonio Canova, that is, after the fall of the First Empire, and after Canova's stay in London, where he admired the Elgin marbles shortly before they were purchased by the British Government from the Earl of Elgin. The *Teseo* was purchased by Emperor Franz I von Habsburg and transferred to Vienna. Ottorino Stefani, *Antonio Canova. La Statuaria* (Milan: Electa, 1999), 121.

23 Fritz Gschnitzer, "Zur Terminologie von ' Gesetz ' und ' Recht ' im frühen Griechisch," in *Kleine Schriften zum griechischen und römischen Altertums*, eds. Catherine Trümpy, Tassilo Schmitt (Stuttgart: Steiner, 2001), 261-268.

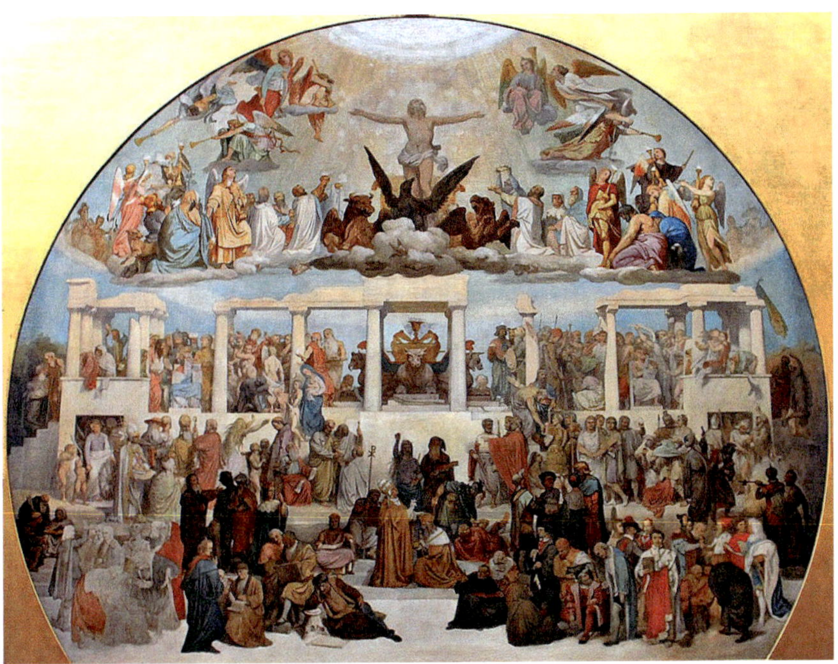

Figure 3.3: Paul Chenavard, *La Palingénésie sociale*. Project for the Pantheon, Paris, commission after 1848. Oil on canvas, 303X381,5 cm. Musée des Beaux-arts, Lyon.

and barbary. Theseus was hailed as a hero founding an ideal Polis, through the adequate use of violence, and through the creation of state institutions.

In fact, Hegelianism provided a new and clear narrative of progress for those who designed imperial museums in Europe. Hegelianism allowed curators to understand that Art was the outcome of a mental process which changed in the course of time, as Humans were evolving towards greater progress. This mental process could be understood thanks to Psychology, when applied to the history of civilisations. In the first stages of History, Humans were hardly conscious of the transformations affecting their mind, but gradually Religion allowed them to grasp this process. In that respect, before the age of science, Art and Religion played a major role; they could fashion the human mind, that is improve, enhance it.

The Hegelian model was anything but neutral. It shaped the contents of universal museums to fit a narrative of progress which could be appropriated by the great imperial nations. It sought to convince visitors that the great empire capable of creating a grand museum had reached the pinnacle of civilization; that therefore, the empire which had founded the museum could pretend to subject the whole world to its rule.

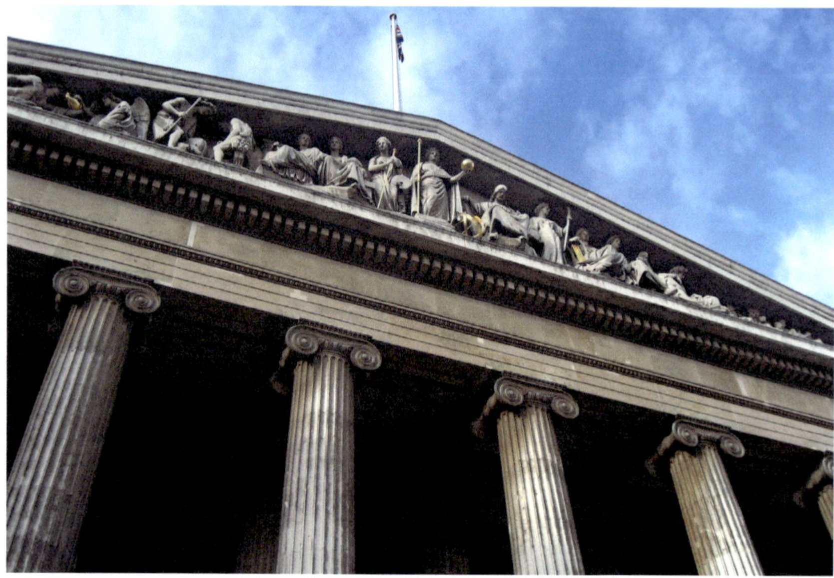

Figure 3.4: Richard Westmacott, *The Progress of Civilization*. Pediment, Main entrance to the British Museum, London. 1851. Figures in the round.

Freud, Moses and the rejection of Universal museums's core ideology

Freud made a profound use of the Kunsthistorisches Museum, and of his collection, in order to produce a phantasmatic vision of history. In effect, Freud condemned Hegelianism both as a historical model and as a museographical argument. The centrepiece of this condemnation is Freud's essay on *Moses*, which was completed in 1934 but published only in 1939.[24] Moses is described by Freud as an Egyptian prince. Ancient Egypt is the first culture where the idea of monotheism is formulated.[25] *Building upon this model, Moses imposed monotheism on the Jews – a choice of huge consequences for Judaism, but also for Christianity and Islam. Giving up the belief in multiple gods forced the Jews to give up their ancient beliefs, which put an enormous psychological strain on their mind. Moses understood the value of this sacrifice; he found a way of soothing their pain, by convincing them that the Jews were God's elected people. When Christianity spread in Europe, Christians took over this by now deep-*

24 A very good and new edition has appeared recently, which contains much unpublished material: Sigmund Freud, *L'Homme Moïse. Un roman historique inédit*, ed., Thomas Gindele (Paris: Imago, 2021); Jacques Le Rider, "L'adieu de Freud à la Grèce : Moïse l'Égyptien," in *Freud, de l'Acropole au Sinaï* (Paris: PUF, 2002), 239- 270.

25 Richard Friedman, *Exodus. How it happened, and why it matters* (Harper Collins, 2017), believes that this idea corresponds to actual historical evidence.

rooted belief that they were God's elected people. Christian bishops and dignitaries tried to exculpate the ancient Romans for having put Christ to death, and to inculpate the Jews for this horrible deed. In the Age of Constantine, the emperor could define the Christian faith as the official religion of the empire, and proclaim himself as a ruler chosen by God to dominate the world. After the breaking up of the Roman Empire, several European kingdoms and empires vied for the status of God's elected people - like France, whose King believed that his kingdom was the 'elder daughter of the Church'.[26] After the Revolution, a disastrous struggle emerged between the most powerful nations, in the same name of a divine election.

Freud's vision of history unearthed the deep, religious roots of imperialism, roots which are so deep that they could even survive the process of secularization, to cause the most horrible destructions in the XXth century. By doing so, Freud questioned the *Telos* of imperial museums and its legitimacy. Thanks to Hegelianism, the Universal museum could raise an imperial capital to the standing of the Centre of the world, marking it with pride as the apex of civilization. Freud, an enthusiastic visitor of the Kunsthistorisches Museum in Vienna, was also the man who wrote the most damning indictment of the imperial museum. His major tool was Psychology, as it was put to the service of the history of civilization. He turned this tool against Hegel. Withdrawn into his own little museum, Freud could rely upon his vast collection of ancient divinities: late at night, he could immerse himself in that magic universe, and project himself into the most distant past when Gods were aplenty, and when the people sought to endear themselves to these Gods.

---

26 Françoise Hildesheimer, *Une brève histoire de l'Eglise. Le cas français (IV-XXIème siècles).* Paris: Flammarion, 2019.

Tulips, Rabies and Books

Cecilia Hurley, Ecole du Louvre/
University of Neuchâtel

"Not a living creature could have anticipated it: but this might be called the grand era of Bibliomania."[1] Thus Thomas Frognall Dibdin commented on the remarkable events at the Roxburghe library sale in London on June 17 1812, when the 1471 Valdarfer edition of Boccaccio's Decameron became the most expensive book yet sold, reaching the price of £2260.[2] The book was reputedly the only extant copy of the *editio princeps* of Boccaccio's masterpiece.[3] Bidding against each other were two cousins – George John, second Earl Spencer and George Spencer-Churchill, fifth duke of Marlborough, marquis of Blandford at the time. Blandford won the day, but his victory was short-lived, and his cousin was to have the last laugh: only seven years later, having run up significant debts by overspending on his famed book collection, Blandford was forced to sell it, including the Valdarfer *Decameron*, which was snapped up for only £918 by none other than the Earl Spencer. The episode and its sequel are pleasantly

1 Thomas Frognall Dibdin, *The Bibliographical Decameron; or, Ten days pleasant discourse upon illuminated manuscripts, and subjects connected with early engraving, typography and bibliography*, 3 volumes, vol. 3 (London: Printed for the Author, 1817), 65.

2 Brian Hillyard, "John Ker, third duke of Roxburghe," in *Pre-nineteenth-century British book collectors and bibliographers*, eds. W. Baker and K. Womack, *Dictionary of Literary Biography*, 213 (1999), 196-206; id., "Ker, John, third duke of Roxburghe (1740-1804), book collector," in *Oxford Dictionary of National Biography*, accessed April 23, 2023, https://www-oxforddnb-com.bnf.idm.oclc.org/view/10.1093/ref:odnb/9780198614128.001.0001/odnb-9780198614128-e-15452; *A Catalogue of the Library of the late John, Duke of Roxburghe* (London: Bulmer and Co., 1812).

3 Giovanni Boccaccio, *Il Decamerone di Giovanni Boccaccio* (Venezia: Christoph Valdarfer, 1471). The copy is now in the Rylands Library, Manchester. There are also copies in London, Paris and Milan, but the Roxburghe copy is the only complete, unmutilated one. The price reached by the Valdarfer in 1812 was not to be surpassed until the sale of a vellum Gutenberg bible in 1873.

piquant but also apposite, illustrating very well not only the high passions but also the considerable fluctuations in book prices that characterised this period.[4] Book-collecting was all the rage and books regularly changed hands at inflated prices. Interest in the printed word, in books in general, and more particularly the passion for old and rare books had been steadily increasing since the early 18th century and reached unheard of proportions in the late Georgian Age.[5] Private libraries were rare in late-17th-century British aristocratic households; by the mid-18th century, however, they were such an indispensable feature of the homes of aristocrats, the wealthy gentry and some of the wealthier members of the liberal possessions, that library furniture and accessories had become very fashionable and were to be had from the best designers.[6] Fifty years later the speculation on books had increased even more, scaling dizzy heights.[7]

The root cause of the excessive prices reached by the Valdarfer Boccaccio, and other books was, according to Dibdin, the 'Bibliomania' that beset his epoch. That Dibdin should have chosen to qualify the Valdarfer episode and the Roxburghe sale as an example of bibliomania would not have unduly surprised many of his bookish contemporaries. He was after all the author of a slim treatise on the subject that had appeared three years earlier entitled *The Bibliomania, or Book-madness*, and that he had then republished in a greatly extended and entirely recast new version, under a slightly different title, only one year before the Roxburghe sale.[8] Just over twenty years

---

4 Ed Potten, "The rest of the iceberg: reassessing private book ownership in the nineteenth century," in *Transactions of the Cambridge Bibliographical Society*, 15/3, *Great collectors and their grand designs: a centenary celebration of the life and work of A. N. L. Munby* (2014), 125-149, 131.

5 Kristian Jensen, *Revolution and the antiquarian book: reshaping the past: 1780-1815* (Cambridge: Cambridge University Press, 2011); David McKitterick, *The invention of rare books: private interest and public memory, 1600-1840* (Cambridge: Cambridge University Press, 2018).

6 Mark Purcell, *The country house library* (New Haven: Yale University Press, 2017); Arnold Hunt, "Private libraries in the age of bibliomania," in *The Cambridge History of Libraries in Britain and Ireland,* eds. Giles Mandelbrote & Keith Manley (Cambridge: Cambridge University Press, 2006) II, 438-458; David Pearson, "Private libraries and the collecting instinct," in *The Cambridge History of Libraries in Britain and Ireland* eds., Alistair Black & Peter Hoare (Cambridge: Cambridge University Press, 2006), III, 180-202.

7 On book sales and book collecting at this time see especially Potten, "The rest of the iceberg", *op. cit.* (note 4); Jon Klancher, "Wild Bibliography: The Rise and Fall of Book History in Nineteenth-Century Britain," in *Bookish Histories: Books, Literature and Commercial Modernity 1700-1900*, eds. Ina Ferris and Paul Keen (Basingstoke: Palgrave Macmillan, 2009), 19-40; Philip Connell, "Bibliomania: Book Collecting, Cultural Politics, and the Rise of Literary Heritage in Romantic Britain," *Representations*, 71 (2000), 24-47; James Raven, *The Business of Books: Book sellers and the English Book Trade* (New Haven: Yale University Press, 2007); William St Clair, *The Reading Nation in the Romantic Period* (Cambridge: Cambridge University Press, 2004).

8 Thomas Frognall Dibdin, *The Bibliomania, or Book-madness, containing some account of the history, symptoms, and cure of this fatal disease. In an epistle addressed to Richard Heber* (London: Longman, Hurst, Rees and Orme, 1809), (87 pages); Thomas Frognall Dibdin, *Bibliomania, or Bookmadness, a bibliographical romance in six parts* (London: Longman, Hurst, Rees, Orme and Brown, 1811), (782 pages). See also Thomas Frognall Dibdin, *Bibliomania or book madness: containing some account of the history, symptoms, and cure of this fatal disease*, ed. Peter Danckwerts (Richmond: Tiger of the Stripe, 2004).

later, when the tide had started to turn, Dibdin's pen was once more at the ready, and he captured the new spirit of the age in his 1832 *Bibliophobia*, an essay bemoaning the waning interest for books.[9] From mania to phobia in only twenty-three years; Dibdin charted the rise and fall of a passion that was to enthral his contemporaries and lead to the excesses that were often seen in auction rooms at the time. Fortunes were made and lost. One seasoned commentator and literary figure of the period, Robert Pearse Gillies, observed that this collecting frenzy, or "bibliographical propensity [...] was nearly as absurd as the *ci-devant* "tulip madness" in Holland."[10]

Dibdin was one of several authors writing about bibliomania in Late Georgian England, who were in turn participating in a much lengthier European tradition. Early texts on the collecting of books include Richard de Bury's *Philobiblon* and the first chapter of Sebastian Brant's *Narrenschiff* (Ship of Fools).[11] But the flowering of the genre, marking a desire on the part of authors across Europe to engage with the concept of bibliomania, occurred during the eighteenth century, when a constellation of texts appeared on the subject. Dibdin was clearly working within this tradition, but he had an effect on the discussion, as will be seen over the following pages. His work to a very great extent contributed to launching the debate in England, where he stamped his mark on bibliomania and on 'bookishness', but also on bibliography, during the late Romantic period. However, as shall be seen, his ideas were much in line with earlier writings by European authors. This essay attempts to examine the figure of Dibdin, as well as his essay and to analyse his contribution to book knowledge in the light of the other texts that had appeared or were appearing.

Dibdin was not solely a keen observer of and commentator on auction houses, book sales and the passions that bibliophilic affairs aroused. Few among his contemporaries would have denied that he also made regular contributions to the literature on book history and bibliophily, even if his writings often qualified him for the title of vulgarizer rather than serious essayist. His work covered a variety of genres, from lists and bibliographies to library catalogues, from essays to bibliographical tours. He also communicated his enthusiasm for books and printed matter through the spoken word, giving three series of lectures during the years 1806-1808 (a total of twenty-eight lectures) at the recently founded Royal Institution.[12] Under the title 'English Literature',

---

9 Thomas Frognall Dibdin, *Bibliophobia, remarks on the present languid and depressed state of literature and the book trade, in a letter addressed to the author of the Bibliomania, by Mercurius Rusticus. With notes by Cato Parvus* (London: H. Bohn, 1832).

10 Robert Pearse Gillies, *Memoirs of a literary veteran; including sketches and anecdotes of the most distinguished literary characters from 1794 to 1849* (London: R. Bentley, 1851), II, 2.

11 The *Philobiblon* was written around 1345 and first published in Cologne in 1473. The *Narrenschiff*, first published in 1494 in Basel, was translated into many languages and appeared in many editions. See Klaus Manger, *Das "Narrenschiff": Entstehung, Wirkung und Deutung* (Darmstadt: Wissenschaftliche Buchgesellschaft, 1983); John Van Cleve, *Sebastian Brant's The ship of fools in critical perspective, 1800-1991* (Columbia: Camden House, 1993).

12 Gwendolen Caroe, *The Royal Institution: an informal history* (London: Murray, 1985).

they offered some insights into the authors of the past although, as Jon Klancher has recently observed, the audience learned less about poetry and prose than about the books as "objects of knowledge", since Dibdin liberally laced his lectures with details on book history, on bibliography and book printing and the history of libraries and book collections.[13] They were undoubtedly part of the range of subjects that Joseph Banks, President of the Royal Society and one of the founders of the Royal Institution, denounced as an effect of "fashion", not in accordance with the original intentions of the Institution.[14] Despite these misgivings, Banks could not deny that the lectures of Dibdin, and others like him, fulfilled one of the Institution's original intentions, namely bringing knowledge in an accessible form to a wide swathe of the population, rich or poor, uneducated or educated, female or male. The Royal Institution drew large audiences and Dibdin must have offered his literary and bibliographical knowledge to a wide and varied public. A sociable and affable figure, doubtless endowed with a silver tongue, Dibdin was a regular presence in literary and bibliophilic gatherings and gained a reputation as an influential figure in fostering and facilitating his age's passion for books, a vocation that he would pursue assiduously and enthusiastically for several years.

Herein lies part of the enigma surrounding Thomas Frognall Dibdin. Persuasive and engaging, he to a large extent overcame his shortcomings. After abandoning a career in law, he took holy orders and found a living paying an annual stipend of less than £200.[15] Keen to supplement his income, he embarked on a constant quest for preferment or for alternative remunerated activities. Writing and publishing seemed initially to offer him an acceptable source of income; they were, however, soon to contribute to his downfall and subsequent acute financial difficulties.

His early forays into the publishing world proved lucrative. In 1802 he produced an *Introduction to the knowledge of rare and valuable editions of the Greek and Roman classics*, which drew heavily on Edward Harwood's earlier work on the

---

13 Jon Klancher, *Transfiguring the arts and sciences: knowledge and cultural institutions in the Romantic age* (Cambridge/New York: Cambridge University Press, 2013), 72-73. See also Ina Ferris, *Book-men, book clubs, and the Romantic literary sphere* (Basingstoke: Palgrave Macmillan, 2015), 67-70. Sarah Zimmerman, *The Romantic Literary Lecture in Britain* (Oxford, Oxford University Press, 2019). Résumés of some of the lectures are to be found in *The Director*, vol. I, 1807, 57-60, 88-91, 155-158.

14 Klancher, *Transfiguring the arts and sciences, op. cit.* (note 13), 63-64.

15 A number of biographies of Dibdin is available: Edward John O'Dwyer, *Thomas Frognall Dibdin: bibliographer and bibliomaniac extraordinary, 1776-1847* (Pinner: Private Libraries Association, 1967); D.A. Stoker, "Thomas Frognall Dibdin", *Nineteenth-century British book-collectors and bibliographers*, eds. W. Baker and K. Womack, DLitB, 184 (1997), 69-80; William Alexander Jackson, *An annotated list of the publications of the Reverend Thomas Frognall Dibdin: based mainly on those in the Harvard College Library, with notes of others* (Cambridge, Mass.: Houghton Library, 1965); Anthony Lister, "George John, 2nd Earl Spencer and his 'librarian', Thomas Frognall Dibdin," in *Bibliophily: Conference: Papers and discussion* eds. Robin Myers and Michael Harris (Cambridge: Chadwyck-Healey, 1986), 90-120; John V. Richardson, "Dibdin, Thomas Frognall (1776-1847), bibliographer", Oxford Dictionary of National Biography, accessed April 23, 2023, https://www-oxforddnb-com.bnf.idm.oclc.org/view/10.1093/ref:odnb/9780198614128.001.0001/odnb-9780198614128-e-7588.

same subject, and which sold out within six weeks. Encouraged by this success, he published three further (enlarged) editions over the next 20 years that earned him several hundred pounds.[16] The *Introduction* also brought him to the attention of the second Earl Spencer, who opened his collections to him, gave him permission to publish the catalogue of them, and even financed the cost of the publication. In all, Dibdin published seven volumes relating to the Spencer collections: five of these were detailed catalogues covering substantial parts of the library, while a further two were devoted to a description of Althorp and all the collections held there (books and artworks).[17] The catalogues were all printed to the highest typographical standards and included much graphic material – plates, facsimiles and illustrations in text. The cost was quite high, but Spencer willingly paid it.

In this context, the episode of the Spencer catalogue is instructive for two reasons. On the one hand, it highlights the strengths and the shortcomings of Dibdin's scholarship. On the other, it reveals his perfectionism and his penchant for high-end, luxury publications, richly illustrated no matter the cost. The question of Dibdin's scholarship is a troubled one, constituting one of the more fascinating and baffling elements of his biography. Through his eloquence and his enthusiasm, he managed to beguile any number of erudite book-collectors, including Spencer, impressing them with the apparent breadth and depth of his knowledge. There was not a rare book, not an early edition – known through many copies or even just one – on which Dibdin could not wax lyrical. He was acquainted with all the great collections and collectors of his epoch – and also of times past. He dispensed this knowledge generously during discussions in lecture halls, in booksellers' shops, in auction rooms, over dinner, in the library of a duke or of an earl. Most importantly, he never shied away from displaying and sharing his learning in one of his many publications. But all too often his enthusiasm outstripped his erudition. From edition to edition, texts grew exponentially: the *Introduction* grew from 63 to 570 pages. The

---

16 Thomas Frognall Dibdin, *An Introduction to the Knowledge of Rare and Valuable Editions of the Greek and Roman Classics: being, in part, a tabulated arrangement from Dr. Harwood's View, &c. With notes from Maittaire, De Bure, Dictionnaire bibliographique, and references to ancient and modern catalogues* (Gloucester: Printed by H. Ruff, 1802); id., *An introduction to the knowledge of rare and valuable editions of the Greek and Latin classics, to which is added a complete Index analyticus, The whole preceded by an account of Polyglot Bibles* (London: for W. Dwyer, 1804). This was followed by several other editions.

17 Thomas Frognall Dibdin, *Bibliotheca Spenceriana; or a Descriptive catalogue of the books printed in the fifteenth century, and of many valuable first editions, in the library of George John Earl Spencer, etc.*, 4 volumes (London: Printed for the Author, 1814-1815); id., *A Descriptive Catalogue of the Books printed in the Fifteenth Century, lately forming part of the library of the Duke di Cassano Serra, and now the property of George John Earl Spencer, K.G. With a general index of authors and editions contained in the present volume, and in the Bibliotheca Spenceriana and Ædes Althorpianæ* (London: Printed for the Author, 1823); id., *Aedes Althorpianae; or an Account of the mansion, books, and pictures, at Althorp; the residence of George John Earl Spencer. To which is added a supplement to the Bibliotheca Spenceriana*, 2 volumes (London: Printed by W. Nicol; sold by Payne & Foss, etc, 1822).

chapters of his books are replete with ungainly digressions and seemingly never-ending footnotes extending over several pages and ostensibly replete with erudition. All too often, however, the scholarship is wanting. Henry Richards Luard, who wrote the biography of Dibdin that appeared in the first edition of the *Dictionary of National Biography*, famously commented that Dibdin could not even read the Greek characters of the titles that he was cataloguing in the Spencer library.[18] Luard was writing some years after Dibdin's death, but his shortcomings had already been identified during his lifetime. *A Bibliographical Antiquarian and Picturesque Tour* published in 1821 offers readers a familiar antiquarian tour in epistolary form abounding with erudite dissertations on printers, bookshops and libraries in the various towns Dibdin visited during a tour of France and Germany.[19] The book is sadly riddled with errors, and French scholars did not hesitate to point this out: they excerpted and translated various parts of Dibdin's text, annotating the text and pointing out all the inaccuracies that spoiled it.[20] Their opinion was often confirmed by Dibdin's compatriots. For example, Alexander Dyce, the editor and literary scholar who was a contemporary of Dibdin, wrote of him some years later that he was "an ignorant pretender without the learning of a schoolboy, who published a quantity of books swarming with errors of every description."[21]

Careless and sloppy Dibdin may have been in terms of the intellectual contents of his works. However, the layout, the quality of the paper and of the facsimile illustrations and the typography could not be faulted. When it came to the production of his books, he was a perfectionist and an aesthete. This habit was to prove ruinous. Earl Spencer generously covered the cost of the printing of the catalogue of his library, even when the project went vastly over budget. Unfortunately for Dibdin, this was an anomaly: he never managed to find another patron generous enough to stump up such large sums of money. As seen above, the *Introduction* earned him several hundred pounds, and he must have hoped to repeat that success on his later projects, thereby guaranteeing a steady supplementary revenue. Sadly, nothing could

18 Luard in his biography of Dibdin in the 1888 edition of the Dictionary of National Biography.

19 Thomas Frognall Dibdin, *A bibliographical, antiquarian and picturesque tour in France and Germany*, 3 vols. (London: Shakespeare Press, 1821).

20 Thomas Frognall Dibdin, *Lettre neuvième relative à la bibliothèque publique de Rouen. Traduite... avec des notes par M. Théodore Licquet*, Paris: de Crapelet, 1821; *id.*, *Lettre trentième concernant l'imprimerie et la librairie de Paris; traduite de l'anglais, avec des notes, par G. A. Crapelet, imprimeur* (Paris: Crapelet, 1821); Mathurin-Marie Lesné, *Lettre d'un relieur français à un bibliographe anglaise* (Paris: Crapelet, 1822); Thomas Frognall Dibdin, *Notice sur les Heures de Charlemagne, mss. de l'an 781, de la Bibliothèque particulière du roi, au Louvre, tirée de la 29e lettre du "Voyage bibliographique, archéologique et pittoresque de M. T. F. Dibdin, en France et en Allemagne", précédée d'un jugement sur l'ouvrage anglais et d'un aperçu de cette bibliothèque, formée en 1814, par M. Barbier* (Paris: Plassan, 1823).

21 Dyce is quoted by Luard in his biography of Dibdin in the 1888 edition of DNB. Before that, the comment appeared in *Bishop Percy's Folio Manuscript*, ... John W. Hales *et al.* ed., 4 vols. (London: N. Trübner & Co, 1867-1868), I, p. liv, note 1.

have been further from the truth. His penchant for working with the best printers and illustrating lavishly his texts proved exorbitant. This extravagance was on occasions compounded by his actions, seemingly those of a man who enjoyed flirting with, almost inviting on himself financial ruin. One anecdote can serve to exemplify this financial recklessness. In 1817, he published his *Bibliographical Decameron*, generally reckoned to be his best work. In this text, a series of staged discussions and debates purportedly held over a period of ten days between six learned friends – Lysander, Belinda, Philemon, Lorenzo, Almansa and Lisardo – allowed Dibdin to demonstrate the mass of bibliographical knowledge that he had been accumulating over the years. The fictitious conversation covers book illustration, printing, book binding, book sales and the history of bibliography, all accompanied by a trove of bookish anecdotes.[22] The literary conceit is clear, but the author manages to pull it off surprisingly well. The book, published in three volumes, is illustrated with a series of wood-block illustrations prepared by the Byfield siblings – Ebenezer, John and Mary – and by William Hughes at considerable cost to Dibdin. A celebratory dinner was held to mark the book's publication, during which Dibdin distributed the original woodblocks to the assembled company; he then enjoined his guests to burn the blocks. Inevitably, no reimpression or new addition of the book would ever be possible, and Dibdin's investment in the materials literally went up in smoke, accompanied by any hope of future profits from a second edition.[23] Admittedly, this is an extreme example of his imprudent attitude to money. Even so, he often lost money on his publications. In a recent article, John Sibbald quite appositely compares Dibdin with a problem or addicted gambler chasing his losses: each new publication was viewed as the chance to recoup his losses on the last one.[24] Needless to say, the much yearned for win never occurred.

In many ways, few people were as well suited as Dibdin to write a text on bibliomania. It is true that his slender means did not allow him to indulge in book collecting on a large scale; he did possess a reference library, that included an impressive number of annotated sale catalogues. But he was afflicted by the condition in many other ways: knowledge about and a passion for books, a need to work with them. It is maybe this fact – that he was passionate about books and about knowledge about them but not consumed by the acquisition of them – that enabled him to write

22 Thomas Frognall Dibdin, *The Bibliographical Decameron or Ten days pleasant discourse upon illuminated manuscripts and subjects connected with early engraving, typography and bibliography*, 3 vols. (London, G. and W. Nicol, 1817).

23 Stoker, "Thomas Frognall Dibdin", *op. cit.* (note 15), p. 77, citing Thomas Frognall Dibdin, *Reminiscences of a literary life*, 2 vols (London: J. Major, 1836), II, 625-630.

24 John A. Sibbald, "Book Bitch to the Rich—the Strife and Times of the Revd. Dr. Thomas Frognall Dibdin (1776-1847)," in *Buying and Selling: The Business of Books in Early Modern Europe*, ed. Shanti Graheli (Leiden: Brill, 2019), 489-521, 498. Dibdin, *Bibliomania*, Danckwerts ed., *op. cit.* (note 8), xxiii.

about the condition as an observer, albeit not entirely dispassionate, and to offer a rather idiosyncratic take on the question.

Much like the *Introduction*, the *Bibliomania* increased considerably in length between the first and the second editions, passing from eighty-seven to more than 780 pages. In fact, the changes are extensive: in the second edition the author adds much extra material, recasts the text almost entirely and also changes the title. The first edition bears the subtitle "history, symptoms and cure of this fatal disease", whereas the second describes itself as a "bibliographical romance in six parts". Accordingly, the first edition is cast as a scholarly dissertation, laid out in three main parts while the second takes the form of a dialogue between six personages – Lysander, Belinda, Philemon, Lorenzo, Almansa and Lisardo – who would later figure in a similar staged dialogue in the *Bibliographical Decameron*. The text in this second edition is organised in six parts, each one set in a recognisable locus for activities relating to books or for discussions on books.[25] This second edition, in its attempt to explain book collecting errs on the side of Dibdin's frequent frailty, namely the tendency to drown his main argument in an ocean of superfluous fact that serves often to deter the reader. This edition in particular attracted the ire of commentators. The reviewer of the *Bibliomania* writing in the *Monthly Review* issued a "most strenuous protest against the heaviness of his text", encumbered as it was by a passion for "notification" (or notes), and felt obliged to mention some but not all of the "numerous list of criticisms that force themselves on almost any reader of the volume".[26] Above all, in this second edition the main tenet of the text, the discussion of the affliction, is almost lost, drowned in superfluous matter. For that reason, the first edition will be studied here.

Interestingly, not once over the eighty-seven pages that he devotes to his subject, does Dibdin define 'bibliomania'. The closest that he comes to a definition is probably one of his assertions in the opening pages of his work when he explains his choices. Here he speaks of "an excessive attachment to any particular pursuit" and then offers a number of comparisons – "horses, hawks, dogs, guns, snuff boxes, old china, coins, or rusty armor".[27] Only a few pages later, the designation of the affliction changes. From an "excessive attachment", an epithet that suggests a rather endearing trait, compulsive perhaps but ultimately benign, bibliomania has now become something more dangerous, a disease. In Dibdin's view, there is one raw truth that needs to be addressed as soon as possible: England is suffering, is in the throes of an illness. "A nation thus glorious, is, at this present eventful moment, afflicted not only with the Dog but the Book disease."[28] Since the illness is prevalent, immediate action is required and Dibdin claims to be able to rise to the situation and offers this short text.

---

25 The evening walk, The Cabinet, The Auction Room, The Library, The Drawing Room, The Alcove.

26 "Art. VI; Bibliomania or Book madness," *Monthly Review* (September-December 1811), 270-283, 271, 279.

27 Dibdin, *The Bibliomania* (1809), *op. cit.* (note 8), 4-5.

28 Dibdin, *The Bibliomania* (1809), *op. cit.* (note 8), 14.

His treatise is couched in medical language, albeit in terms that can easily be understood by laymen, and the text is laid out along the lines of a medical dissertation; three main sections deal with, successively, the history of the illness, its nature and symptoms, then its cure.[29] The structure and the reasoning would have been familiar to anyone who had read treatises such as Richard Manningham's text on Febricula.[30] Further to reinforce the impression that this is an essay that could take its place among the ever increasing corpus of medical literature at the time, Dibdin chooses to conclude it with a synopsis, a device that was a common feature at the end of Renaissance medical texts and inspired by the Ramist tradition.[31] Dibdin explains his decision to use it by reference to Robert Burton's *Anatomy of Melancholy* ("after the manner of Burton, as prefixed to his 'Anatomy of Melancholy'), a compendium of knowledge concerning mental afflictions, first published in 1621 that had come into fashion again at the end of the 18th century.[32]

In the first section, he offers a brief history of book madness or bibliomania, identifying a number of those afflicted with the condition over the last half millennium. More than forty people are introduced here, from Richard de Bury (author of the *Philobiblon*), Henry VII, Sir Thomas More, to a number of Dibdin's near contemporaries. The litany of names draws to a close with that of Reed, presumably the Shakespeare editor and book-collector Isaac Reed who died in 1807. Dibdin scrupulously avoids any mention of a living contemporary, even if the *Bibliomania* is dedicated to Richard Heber, one of the foremost book collectors of the age.[33] The desire to avoid naming his contemporaries becomes more and more understandable as the reader advances through the historical survey. Not once is a collector praised for his efforts, rarely are the beauties or the merits of a collection

---

29 Dibdin, *The Bibliomania* (1809), *op. cit.* (note 8), 14.

30 Richard Manningham, *The symptoms, nature, causes, and cure of the febricula, or, little fever: commonly called the nervous or hysteric fever; the Fever on the Spirits; Vapours, Hypo, or Spleen* (London 1760); Isbrandus de Diemerbroeck, *A Treatise concerning the Pestilence: describing its particular causes, various symptoms, and method of cure ... abridg'd, and translated ... by Thomas Stanton* (London: J. Downing, T. Warner, 1722); Henry Ibbeken, *A treatise on rheumatisms: wherein the nature, causes, and symptoms of rheumatic complaints are explained, and the method of cure laid down* (Dublin: printed by H. Fitzpatrick, 1796); Alun Withey, "Household medicine and recipe culture in eighteenth-century Britain," in *Late Modern English Medical Texts: Writing medicine in the eighteenth century*, eds. Irma Taavitsainen and Turo Hiltunen (Amsterdam/Philadelphia: John Benjamins Publishing Company, 2019), 113-128; Roy Porter, *Bodies politic: disease, death and doctors in Britain, 1650-1900* (London: Reaktion Books, 2001); C. Lawlor, "Introduction: Literature and Medicine in the Long Eighteenth Century," in *Literature and Medicine: The Eighteenth Century*, eds. C. Lawlor & A. Mangham (Cambridge: Cambridge University Press, 2021), 1-20.

31 Dibdin, *The Bibliomania* (1809), *op. cit.* (note 8), 82; David Renaker, "Robert Burton and Ramist Method", *Renaissance Quarterly*, 24, no. 2 (1971), 210-220.

32 Dibdin, *The Bibliomania* (1809), *op. cit.* (note 8), 81.

33 A. Sherbo, "Heber, Richard (1774-1833), book collector," Oxford Dictionary of National Biography, accessed May 15, 2023, https://www-oxforddnb-com.bnf.idm.oclc.org/view/10.1093/ref:odnb/9780198614128.001.0001/odnb-9780198614128-e-12854.

sung; throughout this litany of names, the tone is one of doom as opposed to triumph, resembling a series of cautionary medical tales rather than a history of great English book-collectors. Richard de Bury was "infected with this disease"; Henry VII was a "notorious example of the fatality of the Bibliomania"; John Leland and John Bale did not manage to "escape the contagion"; Spenser was seized with the disorder; it claimed as a victim Harley, Earl of Oxford; Richard Mead's "unrivalled medical skill" could not save either Harley or indeed himself, since he died of the complaint some years after his erstwhile patient.[34] The narrative on countless occasions spills over into the footnotes, where Dibdin bolsters his theory, quoting catalogues, memoirs, savant treatises and gossipy anecdotes in an attempt to prove the devastating ravages of the illness called Bibliomania.

Having offered this interesting but also rather tragic and ominous list of victims, Dibdin then turns in the second section to more practical matters. How does one know if one has succumbed to this condition? A French author, Gabriel Peignot, in his *Dictionnaire raisonné de bibliologie* (1802-1804) suggested that bibliomania is a passion for possessing books and that it amounts to little more than a passion for owning them rather than for reading them.[35] Dibdin considers this far too vague. In his pseudo-medical view, since this is a disease, an illness and not a simple passion, it is indispensable to identify and enumerate the symptoms. He names eight, each of which constitutes an irrefutable sign that the sufferer has indeed contracted bibliomania. They are a desire to own: large paper copies; uncut copies; illustrated copies; unique copies; copies printed on vellum; first editions; true editions; editions printed in black letter.[36] Each of these symptoms is elucidated in greater detail over the course of the following pages. After explaining what a large-paper copy is, Dibdin offers a list of several examples, so that "the sober collector may avoid approaching them". In his view, the passion for large paper copies is a "general and violent" symptom and could well become more prevalent since many books are still published in this form.[37] The other symptoms are then described following this same pattern. Whereas some of them – such as the need to acquire copies printed on vellum – are centuries old, others – for instance the interest in illustrated copies, by which he means the passion for grangerisation, and above all an unmoderated desire to acquire black letter books – are very recent, having spread only in the last decades of the eighteenth century. Many of them can be treated, and if so can be kept in check. The most dangerous, he feels, if not treated quickly and judiciously, is the mania for black-letter copies.[38]

---

34 Dibdin, *The Bibliomania* (1809), *op. cit.* (note 8), 16, 17, 20-21, 28, 29-31.

35 Dibdin, *The Bibliomania* (1809), *op. cit.* (note 8), 57-58; Gabriel Peignot, *Dictionnaire raisonné de bibliologie*, 3 vols, (Paris: Chez Villier, 1802-1804), I, 51: "La bibliomanie est la fureur de posséder des livres, non pas tant pour s'instruire que pour les avoir et pour en repaitre sa vue."

36 Dibdin, *The Bibliomania* (1809), *op. cit.* (note 8), 58.

37 Dibdin, *The Bibliomania* (1809), *op. cit.* (note 8), 58-60.

38 Dibdin, *The Bibliomania* (1809), *op. cit.* (note 8).

After this lengthy and carefully list of symptoms, corroborated by reference to cogent examples, he turns his attention to a possible cure, or cures. As if to appease his readers, he here adopts a more optimistic tone, mulling over the various ways in which the nation can hope to forestall the disease. Despite the fact that "this is a disorder of quite a recent date, and [...] its characteristics, in consequence, cannot be yet fully known or described", he believes that there are five possible antidotes.[39] Rather surprisingly, his first suggestion is that people should actually read more, but only "useful and profitable" works.[40] The idea may seem imprudent, pushing people towards their addiction, but Dibdin feels otherwise. In his view, this will offer an immediate cure to bibliomania as defined by Peignot and by others before him, namely a disease that privileges acquisition over reading of books. In a similar vein, Dibdin suggests that the crazed bidding at auctions could be substantially curbed if rare and useful ("intrinsically valuable") titles were reprinted and if new editions of the best prose authors and poets of the past were to be readily available. His fourth antidote is probably the most interesting, although he glosses over it rather rapidly. He states that the establishment of public institutions can be a powerful remedy, and he indicates the Royal Institution, the Surrey Institution, the London Institution and the Russell Institution, all of which offer their members access to "large libraries of useful books".[41] Finally, and in close relation with these libraries, he recommends that qualified librarians and bibliographers should be appointed, who could select useful books for the libraries and advise and counsel readers.[42] After enumerating and explaining these five antidotes, Dibdin concludes his text with a few sweeping and encouraging comments. While the disease is serious, it is less devastating to the human condition than are many others: "the present one under consideration has the least moral turpitude attached to it" of all the afflictions of human life. His heartfelt hope is that "attending closely to the symptoms of this disorder as they have been described and practising such means of cure as have been recommended, we may rationally hope that its virulence may abate, and the number of its victims annually diminish."[43] He closes the text with the aforementioned synopsis.

It is difficult to know what to make of this text. It has been described correctly as a "slim mock-treatise" that belongs to a "venerable tradition of literary satire".[44] Is it therefore merely a "light-hearted skit" that incited some to join the ranks of the bibliomaniacs, more dangerous than helpful?[45] From there it is easy to dismiss it rapidly, to view it as merely one of several instances of bibliomania, that was

39 Dibdin, *The Bibliomania* (1809), *op. cit.* (note 8), 75.
40 Dibdin, *The Bibliomania* (1809), *op. cit.* (note 8), 76.
41 Dibdin, *The Bibliomania* (1809), *op. cit.* (note 8), 78.
42 Dibdin, *The Bibliomania* (1809), *op. cit.* (note 8), 78-79.
43 Dibdin, *The Bibliomania* (1809), *op. cit.* (note 8), 81-82.
44 Ferris, *Book-men, book clubs, op. cit.* (note 13), 33.
45 Purcell, *The country house library, op. cit.* (note 6), 167.

itself, as Jon Klancher has observed recently, a phenomenon "[l]ong considered a rather clownish sideshow to British literary history".[46] Dibdin's role in bibliomania and more generally bookishness has been much discussed over recent years. There is certainly a satirical tone to the text in places, particularly in the catalogue of illustrious victims in the first part. This is continued to a certain extent in the second and third parts, although here a more censorious attitude becomes evident, betraying the moral and didactic intentions of the author, as is correct for satire. As James Raven has pointed out, the 1809 *Bibliomania* offers some "serious suggestions for 'cures'".[47] It is for that reason that Dibdin's contribution to the debate on bibliomania appears more constructive than, for example, John Ferriar's text that appeared almost contemporaneously.

In his essay, Dibdin refers to only three other texts on the question. On the titlepage he employs an emblematic figure, a vignette showing the book fool famous from Brant's *Ship of Fools*, beneath which are four lines from Alexander Barclay's English translation published by Pynson in 1509.[48] As mentioned above, he quotes Peignot's entry on 'Bibliomanie' in his early nineteenth-century *Dictionnaire*. And there is one further reference to a text on the question, one that had been written and published only a matter of weeks before Dibdin's own text and that was also dedicated to the same bibliophile and book collector, Richard Heber. When informing his readers of his reasons for writing his essay, Dibdin claims that the subject has escaped the attention of all authors except for Dr. John Ferriar.[49] Ferriar, a Scottish poet and physician, published his contribution to the subject in iambic pentameter rhyming couplets in April 1809; Dibdin's text appeared in June 1809.[50] We are to conclude that Dibdin has therefore produced this first version of his text at considerable speed. He admits that when he first saw Ferriar's text he felt simultaneous fear and hope. Fear that he would be one of the principal culprits identified by Ferriar – this feeling of guilt, anticipating some type of moral judgment, would prove to be a very important element in Dibdin's work. Hope, on the other hand, that Ferriar would offer a solution to this debilitating condition. When he read the text, both his fears and his hopes were dissipated.[51] Not only did Ferriar not blame him, he did not even overtly mention

---

46 Klancher, *Transfiguring the arts and sciences, op.cit.* (note 13), 87.

47 James Raven, "Debating Bibliomania and the collection of books in the eighteenth century," *Library and Information History* 29, no. 3 (2013), 196-209, 200.

48 Sebastian Brant, *Shyp of folys of the worlde, Stultifera navis*, Alexander Barclay transl. (London: Printed by Richard Pynson, 1509).

49 John Ferriar, *The Bibliomania, in Epistle to R. Heber* (London, 1809); he republished it in 1812, with a series of other texts. See *The bibliomania by John Ferriar. Bibliography by Thomas Frognall Dibdin: with a synopsis of the symptoms of the bibliomania and a key to Dibdin's "romantic names": two poems edited by Marc Vaulbert de Chantilly* (London: Vanity Press of Bethnal Green, 2001).

50 The dates are to be found in *The Librarian* by James Savage, vol. II, no. 11, 1st May 1809, p. 239, and vol. III, no. 1, 1st July 1809, 46.

51 Dibdin, *The Bibliomania* (1809), *op. cit.* (note 8), 1.

him; nor did he offer any solutions. Dibdin immediately identifies one blatant flaw in Ferriar's text, namely that he has a "pretty strong foresight of the Bibliomania which rages at the present day", but that he does not try to establish any rules for the subject.[52] Ferriar's "persuasive panegyric", he says, is "unmixed, however, with any rules for the choice of books, or the regulation of study".[53] In short, Ferriar does not really offer any answers to the ills of bibliomania. It is true that his verse, while full of references and allusions to many of the great texts, authors and printers, offers a far less measured and reasoned account than does Dibdin's. In effect, he identifies only a few of the symptoms. Above all, he offers no advice, no treatment, no antidotes, or cures; his work is little more than a flight of fantasy. He subscribes to the theory that this is merely a form of madness.

Dibdin mentions only three other texts on bibliomania. Given his extensive, one is almost tempted to say exhaustive, bibliographical knowledge, this may well seem a little disingenuous, since texts there certainly had been over the course of the preceding decades and even centuries. It is true that little had been written on the subject in English before Ferriar and Dibdin, at least nothing of comparable length dealing with the subject in such detail.

Nevertheless, as some authors have recently observed, the word was not completely unfamiliar by the end of the opening decade of the nineteenth century.[54] The word seems to have been employed in English by Thomas Hearne as early as 1734, no doubt coined after the French term 'bibliomanie', apparently first employed by Guy Patin in 1654. Occasional occurrences are to be found, but the word gained greater parlance during the closing decades of the eighteenth century. In England, Edward Harwood offered a definition of it in his work on Greek and Roman literature (1775), saying that: "The knowledge of books, like the knowledge of every art that is arduous and useful, must be purchased at a high price; and can only be acquired by an assiduous and judicious application to this pursuit for a considerable number of years. Some, indeed, whom God has blessed with more opulence than understanding, burn with an insatiable ardour of enjoying every beauteous form of a favourite book that hath ever been exhibited in any country since the invention of the typographical art; and others have the Bibliomania in so dire and frantic a degree, that those rare Editions, which they despair of securing by their wealth, they will not hesitate about secreting from libraries by their ingenuity."[55] In 1791, Isaac Disraeli warned that bibliomania, "the collecting an enormous heap of books" has

---

52 Dibdin, *The Bibliomania* (1809), *op. cit.* (note 8), 9.

53 Dibdin, *The Bibliomania* (1809), *op. cit.* (note 8), 2.

54 McKitterick, *The Invention of Rare Books*, *op. cit.* (note 5), 250-268: Books in Turmoil, 250. Raven, "Debating Bibliomania", *op. cit.* (note 47); Connell, "Bibliomania", *op. cit.* (note 7).

55 Edward Harwood, *A view of the various editions of the Greek and Roman classics, with remarks* (London: printed for G.G.J. and J. Robinson, 1790); p. v. Dibdin's own 1802 bibliography of classical authors owed much to Harwood, and he acknowledged his debt to his predecessor in the title.

been "the rage with some who would fain pass themselves upon us for men of vast erudition".[56] A short article on the books from the Strawberry Hill Press appeared in *The Monthly Mirror* in July 1798 under the title of 'Bibliomania'.[57] There were also other texts that included the word, usually explaining it with a desultory reference to the desire to acquire may books during this same period.

European authors were more prone to write on the question.[58] The bibliomaniac figured, of course, in Sebastian Brant's *Ship of Fools*, as the person who keeps useless books but knows nothing about their contents, establishing in the European tradition the figure of the person crazy to acquire and possess books, however useful or useless they may be. The eighteenth century witnessed a number of texts on the subject, some of which addressed the topic in considerable detail. In 1761, Louis Bollioud de Mermet, a musicographer from Lyons, published under the address of The Hague a text devoted to bibliomania.[59] The treatise extends to 111 octavo pages, making it the longest text on the question that had appeared to that date. Mermet opens with an observation that sets him firmly in the tradition of Brant's comments on the Book Fool, namely that bibliomania is a desire to possess books, even if they will never be read. Over the course of the treatise he does, however, develop a number of ideas that would also find a place in later texts including, notably, Dibdin's. Far from contenting himself with vague enunciations about the dangers of a passion for books, he attempts to enumerate the various manifestations of the passion for books, identifying a desire to acquire incunabula, rare or unique copies, uncut copies, large paper copies, unusual copies, different formats of the same text, richly illustrated books and opulent bindings. Many if not all of the categories that he mentions prefigure those identified by Dibdin. Furthermore, Mermet inserts a passage on the importance of libraries, explaining how they can offer scholars the possibility to acquaint themselves with books on many subjects without ruining themselves. He also rounds off his text with a series of recommendations, or "précautions" as he terms them. These are not as pointed and constructed as are Dibdin's cures; they can be encapsulated in the advice to read less and to read more profitably. Contrary to Dibdin's *Bibliomania*, Mermet's text is by no means what could be described as satirical. His tone is far more serious, verging regularly on the censorious and moralistic; his chief complaint is that people are ruining themselves and that they have abandoned any show of moderation and restraint. He is highly critical of his

---

56 Isaac Disraeli, *Curiosities of literature: Consisting of anecdotes, characters, sketches, and observations, literary, critical, and historical* (London: printed for J. Murray, 1791), 19.

57 "Bibliomania", *The Monthly Mirror*, vol. 6, July 1798, 297.

58 See especially, Alexander Košenina, *Der gelehrte Narr: Gelehrtensatire seit der Aufklärung*, Göttingen: Wallstein-Verlag, 2003, pp.133-152: Bibliomanie oder der gelehrte Wahn; Alberto Castoldi, *Bibliofollia*, Bruno Mondadori, Milano, 2004; Ugo Rozzo, *Furor bibliographicus, ovvero la bibliomania* (Macerata: Biblohaus, 2011).

59 Louis Bollioud de Mermet, *De la bibliomanie*, (La Haye), 1761; a reprint appeared in 1765.

contemporaries, and describes their descent into immoderate book-buying, soon followed by "honteuse déroute", their shameful utter defeat.[60] Interestingly, he does from time to time in his text offer a slight variation on this theme, stating that his contemporaries are victims of or even "martyrs" to an illness, that he equates with hydropsy, remarking at one point that "Il me semble de voir un hydropique que rien ne désaltère".[61] The image is striking, since Dibdin would also employ a similar image of physical illness in his discussion of the affliction.

Mermet was not alone in devoting a lengthy text to the question of bibliomania. Three university dissertations appeared on the question during the eighteenth century.

In 1715, Johann Jacob Rohde presented a dissertation at Königsberg on the question of scholars who had bought and collected too many books.[62] Rohde quotes many examples of such figures, and concludes that libraries are very useful, while maintaining that careful selection of books is necessary and that they should be assembled for study purposes rather than for show or personal glory.[63] Rohde does not employ any medical language, nor does he speak of a craze or an illness. Above all, the word 'bibliomania' is absent from his text. Some years later, the word was to the fore when, in 1739, Johann Friedrich Reitz, a doctor in literature and medicine who became professor of history and rhetoric at the University of Utrecht, gave a speech in Utrecht on Bibliomania.[64] He identified it as an endemic disease, defining it as the "frenzy for books" or "the insatiable urge to possess or to write many books."[65] His medical training encourages him to approach this scientifically and he therefore proposes to examine the causes, the symptoms, the prognosis and the treatment, much as Dibdin would do some seventy years later. The causes are twofold: people believe that books contain all the knowledge that they will ever need, and booksellers encourage people to buy. There are several symptoms, including spending more time visiting bookshops than sitting in libraries, an irrepressible urge to read book catalogues and to identify desiderata, an urge to purchase books even if one is of an advanced age and will have to dispose of them very soon. The prognosis is less than rosy, all the more so because it is always harder to treat people who are afflicted with

60 Mermet, *Bibliomanie, op. cit.* (note 59), 85.

61 "I get the impression that I see someone afflicted by hydropsy, who cannot slake his thirst": Mermet, *Bibliomanie, op. cit.* (note 59), 57.

62 Johann Jacob Rohde, *Dissertatio Historico-Moralis, De Eruditorum Nimio Libros Coemendi Congerendique Studio, Sive: Von dem unmäßigen Bücher-Kauff der Gelehrten : A. R. S. MDCCXV. ad diem X. Jul.*, Königsberg: Reusner, 1715.

63 Rohde, *Dissertatio Historico-Moralis, op. cit.* (note 62), 26-27.

64 Johan Frederik Reitz, *Joan. Fred. Reitzii Oratio de bibliomania habita a. d. 7 id. septembr. 1739 quum... Carolus Richard ac Theodorus van Romondt ad academiam dimittendi pro venatione et in venationem pro concione essent dicturi* (Utrecht: A. Van Megen, 1739); K.A. Manley, "Blurred lines in the history of domestic libraries in the age of Dibdin's Bibliomania," in *Libraries, Books, and Collectors of Texts, 1600-1900*, eds. Annika Bautz, James Gregory (New York: Routledge, 2018), 231-245, 234.

65 Reitz, *Oratio, op. cit.* (note 64), 3 (endemic), 4 (frenzy).

a disease of the mind or spirit rather than a physical one. As for the cure, it is based on two actions. First, potential sufferers should learn to distinguish between useful and useless books. Secondly, they should beware the tricks of booksellers.[66]

Reitz speaks about a disease but situates it in the mind or the spirit. Twenty-three years later, Andreas Wallin offered his contribution to the question in a thesis that he defended at Uppsala.[67] He adopts a more etymological approach in his work than Reitz, and also draws far more heavily on Early Modern authors who have written on studying and on books. He defines bibliomania as "an intemperate lust for accumulating books, akin to madness", and feels that very often the books are not used. The term can also be extended to reading, writing as well as collecting books.[68] Wallin offers advice on reading – suggesting that people should read well rather than a lot.[69] He devotes several pages to a discussion of the use that can be made of good libraries. On the other hand, his text offers less in the way of identification of the symptoms and the possible cure for what is, in his eyes, a form of madness. In 1802, in his dictionary, Peignot codifies much of the earlier thought on bibliomania, although he does not reveal any interest in the medical approach to the condition. He offers as we have seen a definition of bibliomania that once again highlights the immoderate desire for acquisition and possession.[70] He even describes the mania as ridiculous. Notably, he identifies very few bibliomaniacs, and only people living in ancient times.

Several texts addressing bibliomania had been published in the eighteenth century. Quite how far these had circulated is not entirely clear, and it is maybe unfair to imagine that Dibdin could have had access to all or even some of them, despite his impressive bibliographical knowledge. There is, however, one text that Dibdin did not mention although he could have been expected to know it. In Diderot and d'Alembert's *Encyclopédie* feature two articles, one on the figure of the bibliomaniac and one on the condition known as bibliomania. The bibliomaniac, says the author of the article, familiar to us from La Bruyère's *Caractères* (quoted at length in the article) is possessed by a craze or madness that leads him to buy books without needing them: "Il a des livres pour les avoir, pour en repaître sa vûe."[71] The article on bibliomania does not go so far as to propose a cure, but does observe that there are only two justifiable reasons for purchasing books. The first of these is to

66 Reitz, *Oratio*, *op. cit.* (note 64), 9.

67 Andreas J. Wallin, *Dissertatio Academica, De Bibliomania, Quam, Venia Incliti Collegii Philosophici, Ad Regium Upsaliense Lyceum, Sub Præsidio Mag. Petri Ekerman, Eloqu. Profess. Reg. Et Ord. Publico Examini Offert Alumnus Regius, Andreas J. Wallin, Sudermannus. In Aud. Carol. Maj. Ad Diem III. Aprilis, Anni MDCCLXII*, Uppsala, 1762.

68 Wallin, *De Bibliomania*, *op. cit.* (note 67), 4.

69 Wallin, *De Bibliomania*, *op. cit.* (note 67), 5.

70 Peignot, *Dictionnaire raisonné*, *op. cit.* (note 35), I, 51-52.

71 Article "Bibliomane", in Denis Diderot & D'Alembert, *Encyclopédie, ou Dictionnaire raisonné des sciences, des arts et des métiers*, 35 vols. (Paris: Briasson, 1751-1780), II, 228. The phrase was then reused by Peignot in his *Dictionnaire*.

buy them because of what they contain, and to be able to read them accordingly, using what is intelligent and useful and laughing off what is foolish or incorrect. The second of these is to purchase a large number of books and to allow other people and scholars to read and consult them.[72]

Some years later, and only two years before Ferriar and Dibdin published their texts, another contribution to the debate had appeared, this time in Italian. The author was a great book collector, the Count Leopoldo Cicognara.[73] Cicognara had not only read Diderot and D'Alembert's text, but he also drew on it considerably in his essay. The circumstances of this essay are interesting. Cicognara recounts that he had managed to find an extremely rare opuscule, the *Vita di S. Lazzaro Monaco e Pittore* first published in 1681. Knowing that many people were looking for a copy of the work, he at first decided to publish a counterfeit version of it. However, he thought better of this and finally chose to republish it with a lengthy preface on the nature and the dangers of bibliomania. In effect, Cicognara draws heavily on the Encyclopaedists' articles, and stresses that the use that can be made of books should be more important than the mere fact of owning them. He speaks vaguely about bibliomania as an illness, but does not couch his essay in medical terms. He does not identify 'symptoms' although he does explain the various types of books that bibliomaniacs want to purchase. Above all, he insists on the fact that books should be chosen carefully and should be used. He may not use the word 'bibliophile', but his general meaning is much the same as Peignot's (and the Encyclopaedists' before him): purchasing books, even beautiful and precious ones, is permissible, as long as they are going to be used by the purchaser or by someone else.

As this rapid survey shows, there had certainly been literature on the subject before Dibdin set about writing his text, only some of which we can be sure that he knew. Various authors had set out a range of theories on bibliomania and of possible responses to the condition. Some, such as Mermet, preferred to occupy the moral high ground, while others, such as Reitz, took a more dispassionate, mock medical approach to it. In the light of this, Dibdin's choices inspire comment. One interesting feature sets the British contributions – not only Ferriar and Dibdin's, but also those of their predecessors – apart from the more recent European literature. The article immediately following 'Bibliomanie' in Peignot's dictionary is entitled 'Bibliophile'.[74] Here, the author explains that it would be judicious to distinguish

---

72 Article "Bibliomanie", in Denis Diderot & D'Alembert, *Encyclopédie, ou Dictionnaire raisonné des sciences, des arts et des métiers*, 35 vols. (Paris: Briasson, 1751-1780), II, 228.

73 Leopoldo Cicognara, *Vita di S. Lazzaro, monaco e pittore (pubblicata da Lazzaro Baldi), preceduta da alcune osservazioni sulla bibliomania*, Brescia: N. Bettoni, 1807. Cicognara's collection books is known through the catalogue: Leopoldo Cicognara, *Catalogo ragionato dei libri d'arte e d'antichità posseduti dal conte Cicognara*, 2 vols. (Pisa: N. Capurro, 1821). See Elena Granuzzo, "Leopoldo Cicognara and his library: Formation and significance of a collection (I)," *Journal of Art Historiography*, 27 (2022), 1-45.

74 Peignot, *Dictionnaire raisonné*, *op. cit.* (note 35), I, 52-53.

between the bibliomaniac and the booklover since the latter seeks out useful books, that will be useful for their studies, and is guided by intellectual considerations rather than by a blind passion for acquisitions.[75] The distinction is made clearly and is explained well.

It is thus all the more surprising that Dibdin did not attempt to exploit the semantic opportunities proposed by the French language and explained by Peignot and try to soften his voluble criticism of bibliomaniacs by pointing out that there is a milder, tamer version of the love for books and the desire to possess them that can be qualified as bibliophily. It is true that Dibdin did employ the word book-lover in his treatise, but he immediately subsumed it into the category of bibliomaniacs, thereby effectively negating its use as a word referring to commendable consumers of the written word: "It may be expected that I should notice a few book-lovers, and probably Bibliomaniacs, previously to the time of Richard De Bury."[76] In fact, the word bibliophile (and bibliophilism) does not enter the English language until 1824 in a text by Dibdin, referring to the French society of book-lovers (Société des bibliophiles).[77] Dibdin's decision to turn a blind eye to this term is all the more intriguing since the bibliophile would seem in many ways to correspond to the reasonable figure who adopts a more measured attitude to books as presented in the last part of his *The Bibliomania*.

Book-collecting as it was practised in England at the turn of the nineteenth century would appear, in the texts written by Ferriar and Dibdin, to be considered to be a reprehensible activity. Dibdin knew the collectors of his time well, and the list of symptoms that he gave was accurate. Large paper, first editions, illustrated copies and black letter texts were becoming more and more sought after. However, and this is a further intriguing element of Dibdin's theory, that marks him off from not only the British but also the European authors who wrote on the question, he does seem reluctant to attribute too much blame to the bibliomaniacs. He does not diminish their guilt by suggesting that they are bibliophiles rather than bibliomaniacs. What he does do, rather, is to plead mitigating circumstances, explaining that they are not entirely responsible for their actions. He shifts the onus from them and their personal guilt to an unidentified but potent external force, by stating that bibliomania is an illness, but a physical rather than a mental one.

The phrase in which Dibdin explains his theory is all too easily missed: "A nation thus glorious, is, at this present eventful moment, afflicted not only with the Dog but the Book disease."[78] The author is no doubt referring to English nation's

---

75 Peignot, *Dictionnaire raisonné, op. cit.* (note 35), I, 52: "celui qui, dirigé par le seul désir de s'instruire, aime et se procure les bons ouvrages, qu'il croit les plus propres à composer une collection intéressante par le nombre et par la variété des articles."

76 Dibdin, *The Bibliomania* (1809), *op. cit.* (note 8), 16.

77 Thomas Frognall Dibdin, *The Library companion, or the Young man's guide and the old man's comfort, in the choice of a library* (London: Harding, Triphook, and Lepard, 1824), 4.

78 Dibdin, *The Bibliomania* (1809), *op. cit.* (note 8), 14.

infamous fondness for dogs as pets; this reading seems all the more likely given that earlier in the text, when defining bibliomania, he stated that it corresponds to “an excessive attachment to any particular pursuit” and then offers a number of comparisons – “horses, hawks, dogs, guns, snuff boxes, old china, coins, or rusty armor”.[79] But Dibdin is in fact thinking of something very particular, as he indicates in the corresponding footnote where we find a reference to a recent dissertation by Benjamin Moseley on Hydrophobia – or rabies.[80] Little was known for sure about the illness at the time, and it inspired some colourful theories on the nature and origins of the condition.[81] Moseley, examining several cases, tried to establish the causes, the symptoms and the possible cure.

By means of this simple allusion to rabies, Dibdin disculpates the bibliomaniacs. Bibliomania is not a psychological condition, in any way self-induced, but a physiological one. The bibliomaniac is not a culprit but an innocent victim: attacked by an external organism, akin to a bacterium. Dibdin does not explain how it is transmitted – whether by the bite of a dog, or another animal, or whether it is airborne. What is certain, however, is that Dibdin the clergyman, by means of this comparison with the dog disease, managed to a great extent to exonerate his fellow bibliomaniacs. Impulsive and excessive collecting, the unruly passion, was here compared with animalistic impulses.[82] The book fool described in Brant's *Ship of Fools* – featuring in the vignette on Dibdin's title page – was, by means of some sophistic pseudo-medical reasoning transformed into the human equivalent of a rabid dog.

---

79 Dibdin, *The Bibliomania* (1809), *op. cit.* (note 8), 4-5.

80 Benjamin Moseley, *On Hydrophobia, its prevention and cure. With a description of the different stages of canine madness. Illustrated with cases* (London: Longman, 1808).

81 Lise Wilkinson, “Understanding the Nature of Rabies: An Historical Perspective”, in *Rabies*, J.B. Campbell & K.M. Charlton eds. (Boston: Springer, 1988) (Developments in Veterinary Virology, vol 7), 1-23; Bill Wasik & Monica Murphy, *Rabid: a cultural history of the world's most diabolical virus* (New York: Penguin Books, 2013).

82 Werner Muensterberger, *Collecting: an unruly passion: psychological perspectives* (Princeton: Princeton University Press, 1994).

How to Form a *Wunderkammer* in 1600

The Encyclopedic Collection of Bernardus Paludanus (1550-1633)

Marika Keblusek, Leiden University

In September 1592, travelling from England back home to Stuttgart, Friedrich, duke of Württemberg and Teck, stayed overnight in Enkhuizen.[1] The next day, after climbing the town's tower to enjoy a view of the Zuiderzee, Friedrich was given a tour through the museum of Bernardus Paludanus, the town's physician. Friedrich's inscription in Paludanus's *album amicorum* testifies to this occasion.[2]

In his *Warhaffte Beschreibung Zweyer Reise* [True Account of Two Trips] (published in 1603-4), Jakob Rathgeb, the duke's secretary, included a report on this

> Wunderkammer, which can truthfully be called a Wunderkammer or miracle room, because he [*ie* Paludanus] has such wonderful things, which he himself has brought over from India and Egypt, and other far away strange lands, things which would not quickly be found anywere else together. And of each object a description will now follow, for the sake of wonder.[3]

---

1 Parts of this essay are taken from my forthcoming article in Elizabeth Harding and Joelle Weis (eds), *Objekt:Listen. Medialität von Dingverzeichnissen in der Frühen Neuzeit*.

2 National Library, The Hague (KB); MS 133 M 63, fol. 23r.

3 Jakob Rathgeb, *Warrhafte Beschreybung zweyer Raisen, welcher erste (die Badenfahrt genannt) der Durchleuchtig Hochgeborne Fürst unnd Herr, Herr Friderich Hertzog zu Württemberg unnd Teckh*

Using the term *Wunderkammer* (room of wonders, or, cabinet of curiosities), Jakob Rathgeb referred to the type of collections that had become a staple at German princely courts by the end of the sixteenth century. Whether in Dresden, Münich or Kassel, these so-called *Kunst- und Wunderkammern* typically contained large quantities of beautiful objects made by craftsmen (*artificialia*: Kunst) and precious and strange things found in nature (*naturalia*: Wunder). Other "categories", such as *exotica* (objects from Asia, Africa and the Americas) and *scientifica* (scientific instruments) hint at the hybrid and overlapping character of these *Kunst- und Wunderkammer* classifications: an exotic rare thing from nature (say, a piece of coral, ivory or a coconut) was often transformed by craftsmen like engravers or goldsmiths to become a new, stunning piece of decorative art.

Of course, collecting as a phenomenon in Europe did not have its origins in the early modern period. But the opening up of the non-European world, as well as the invention of the printing press, had brought strange, exciting, frightening and most of all unknown objects and information into Europe from the late 15th century onwards – which in turn changed the existing medieval religious and secular cultures of collecting. Scholars of natural history tried to reconcile the existence of formerly unknown plants or species – whether the bird of paradise, the armadillo, or the rhinoceros – with the *sapientia*, the ancient wisdom gathered from classical authors (such as Aristotle, Dioscorides or Pliny) as well as from the Bible. These scholars, often with a medical background, now set up impressive collections, trying to encompass the "whole world" or the "materials of nature" in their studies and libraries by collecting what also was referred to as "wonderful" things.[4]

Thus, "for the sake of wonder", 23 unpaginated pages were inserted in the *Warhaffte Beschreibung* of duke Friedrich's visit. They contain the first inventory or catalogue of the Paludanus collection, specifically (but not exclusively) of the *res omnia naturalia*: that is, "all the things from nature". Bernardus Paludanus had been born in Steenwijk, Overijssel, as Berent ten Broecke in 1550, and had lived abroad from the early 1570s onwards.[5] In 1573 he enrolled at the university of Heidelberg and from *c.*1576 continued his academic studies in Padua, where he would obtain his medical doctorate in 1580. During his study years, Paludanus visited many cities in

---

[...] im Jahr 1592 von Mümppelgart auß, in das weitberühmte Königreich Engellandt: hernach im zuruck ziehen durch die Niderlandt biß widerumb gen Mümppelgart, wol verrichtet: die ander, so Hochgemelter Fürst auß [...] Studtgarten, im Jahr 1599 in Italiam gethan, und von Rom auß, durch vil andere Ort, widerumb gen Studtgart, anno 1600 im Mayen, glücklich heimgelangt, Tübingen 1604, fol. 42v.

4 See Eric Jorink, *Reading the Book of Nature in the Dutch Golden Age, 1575-1715*, Leiden 2010; Paula Findlen, *Possessing Nature. Museums, Collecting, and Scientific Culture in Early Modern Italy*, Berkeley 1996.

5 A biography of Paludanus in H. Hunger, 'Bernardus Paludanus (Berent ten Broeke) 1550-1633. Zijn verzamelingen en zijn werk', in: J.H. van Linschoten, *Itinerario*, ed. C.P. Burger, III, The Hague 1934, pp. 249-268. I am working on a new biography, to be included in my book on the Paludanus album and his collections, *Paper Worlds*.

Italy, travelled to the islands of Malta and Sicily, and spent four months in the Holy Land and Egypt. Between 1580 and 1581, he toured extensively in Germany, from Strasbourg, Augsburg and Innsbruck, to Jena, Leipzig, Braunschweig and Bremen. After his return to his home country, initially to Zwolle and in 1586 to Enkhuizen where he was appointed as the town's physician, he only occasionally travelled abroad, visiting London in 1591-1592, and Hesse in 1597 and 1600. In 1633, at the age of 83, Paludanus died in Enkhuizen; two years later an epitaph was installed in the Zuiderkerk, commemorating the way his collection comprised objects from four parts of the world: Asia, Europe, Africa, and the kingdom of Nature.

Paludanus's use of the title *Index* as a key to his collection is revealing. In a sense, this is a sort of *visual* catalogue, for the objects, arranged according to material – stones, minerals, shells *etc* – are depicted in the drawers that contain them. Grids and tables were certainly used in botanical, medical and pharmaceutical publications, but I have not come across any other contemporary catalogue in which these were similarly used to visually index a collection.[6] By using this form of visual representation, the drawers are here depicted as if the reader has just opened one and is looking into it from above, seeing all the subdivisions (boxes) at once. Alluding to the performative aspect of collections, this visual cataloguing enabled a reader not only to imagine himself as an active participant in the physical space of the museum, but also allowed him to have an immediate overview of the general and the specific of a certain sort of thing – in other words, to *visually understand* the classification of specific parts of nature.

Yet it is hard to imagine exactly what the Paludanus museum must have looked like and to determine how many objects were preserved there. The *Index* counts 87 so-called large drawers, probably stored in cabinets (these are not explicitly mentioned). These drawers are then divided in "boxes", "little drawers", or "little cabinets", holding a single object (such as a shell or a piece of wood) or groups of objects and materials (several stones or "sand from India"). There are three groups: the first 40 drawers (divided in 2096 boxes) are filled with objects and material "from the earth and made by fossils"; drawers 41 to 66 (divided in 1665 boxes) contain "things belonging to the garden, in and on the earth", while the third group of "things from the water and the sea" has twenty large drawers made up from 1845 boxes. All in all, this makes for a minimum of 5600 objects. Paludanus's interest in ethnographic *exotica* is evident from the last item in the catalogue; a drawer "containing diverse costumes (*Kleydung*) and foreign things from Syria, Persia, Armenia, the East and West Indies, Turkey, Arabia and Moscow, several hundreds of them".

The index was drawn up by Paludanus himself, and then published in the *Warhaffte Beschreybung*, providing an idea of the collection's vast size and scope

---

6 See Claudia Swan, 'From Blowfish to Flower Still Life Paintings. Classification and Its Images, circa 1600', in: Pamela H. Smith and Paula Findlen (eds), *Merchants & Marvels. Commerce, Science, and Art in Early Modern Europe*, New York / London 2002, pp. 109-136.

around 1592. Three later catalogues – drawn up by Paludanus in 1600, in 1617 and in 1624 respectively – confirm these already staggering numbers and in fact show how the collection grew even larger in the course of time, containing dried fruits, leaves, plants; diverse sorts of local and tropical woods; stuffed birds (including birds of paradise and parrots); prepared fish and reptile skins; drawers filled with insects, shells, mussels and corals; animal bones, horns and antlers; boxes full of earth and clay specimens, stones, gems, minerals and large pieces of marble and coral; an extensive collection of antique and contemporary medals, and coins of foreign currencies in gold, silver and copper; "exotic" spears, knives and swords, as well as items of clothing and utensils from "both Indies"; Chinese writing tools and Egyptian mummies.[7]

Around 1620, Paludanus's rooms in Enkhuizen held 400 ethnographic objects from Asia, the Americas and Africa; 8700 shells; 1900 seeds and plants; 3400 minerals and fossils. The collection numbered at least 17.000 items. Indeed, his cabinet was the most extensive and influential collection of *naturalia* and *exotica* in the Dutch Republic around 1600 and can be considered the starting point of Dutch collecting history. In this paper, I would like to further explore the various ways and means Paludanus used to enlarge, to maintain and to manage his museum – and thus draw attention to the logistics and practicalities of collecting in the 1600s.

It is likely that Paludanus was inspired to develop a collection during his student years in Padua, from 1576 to 1580, and that a great number of objects were gathered by himself during his extensive travels – the first of four main ways to enlarge a collection, followed by donation, exchange and purchase.

During his time in Padua, Paludanus visited Rome, Naples and Bologna where he met the most notable naturalists-collectors of the time, like Ferrante Imperato, Francesco Calzeolari and in particular Ulisse Aldrovandi, whom he would later reverentially refer to as my "tutor".[8] Physicians and apothecaries like Aldrovandi and Imperato at the time were highly invested in keeping gardens and collecting natural materials – *materia medica* – which their profession required. As Paula Findlen has shown, in Italy especially medical professionals assembled large museums as an essential part of the changing scientific culture in the mid-1500s.[9] These museums must have inspired Paludanus to expand his own collection of

---

7 Thus far, four different inventories/catalogues of the Paludanus collection are known: Rathgeb, see note 2 (1592, published in 1603-4); Carpentras, Bibliothèque Inguimbertine, MS 1821, f. 333r-340v (1600); Kopenhagen, Kongelige Bibliotek (KKB), MS GKS, 3467, 8^{0} (1617); Florence, Biblioteca Laurenziana, coll. Ashburnham 1828 (1624). For a more elaborate discussion of these see my forthcoming essay 'Listing the Wunderkammer. Order and Narrative in Catalogues of the Paludanus-Collection, c. 1600,' in: Elizabeth Harding and Joelle Weis (eds), *Objekt:Listen. Medialität von Dingverzeichnissen in der Frühen Neuzeit*.

8 KB, MS 133 B 63, fols. 245v; 248r; 249r; Florence, Biblioteca Laurenziana, coll. Ashburnham 1828, fol. 10r.

9 See Findlen, *Possessing Nature*, passim.

natural specimens which as an inspiring physician he most certainly was investing in. His first professional objects, then, were related to plant materials, yet he was clearly interested in the budding field of geology as well.

From inscriptions in his *album amicorum*, we know that Paludanus visited the islands of Malta and Sicily, where he collected lava fragments and stones from the surroundings of the Vesuvius, as he had previously done near the Etna. Between 1580 and 1581, he travelled extensively in Germany with a particular interest in the mining areas in Saxony and Bohemia: Glachau, the birthplace of Agricola, Annaberg Bucholz and Joachimsthal. According to his letters, he was sometimes allowed to enter a mine and extract minerals and ores himself – and these items were indeed mentioned in the *Index* published by Rathgeb. Similarly, objects which Paludanus collected during his four months travel in the Holy Land and Egypt (leaving from Venice on 21 June and returning there on 11 October 1578) made it into his collection, for example "relics brought back from Jerusalem and Rome", "little stones from Mount Sion near Jerusalem, where Christ had the Last Supper" or "a little stone from the top of the Olive Mountain where Christ the Lord has ascended into Heaven, where one can see one of His footsteps". Several Egyptian amulets excavated by Paludanus himself in the necropolis of Saqqara by "cracking open the dead bodies" were also added to the collection.[10]

Early modern collectors like Paludanus, who built up private cabinets, to a large extent were also dependent on patrons and friends who would donate or exchange objects. The importance of gift giving and gift display in the early modern period has been well documented and studied, for example by Mario Biagioli, Sharon Kettering and Paula Findlen. As Findlen has argued, "collectors offered patrons multiple ways to express their devotion to them as clients: gifts, visits ... all contributed to the splendor of the museum and its creator. In return, they showered princes with numerous signs of their devotions".[11] We can see this clearly on the Paludanus portrait by Hendrick Gerritsz Pot (1629), which shows him with a gold portrait medal pendant of Maurits, prince of Orange, with whom he exchanged letters on antiquities.[12]

Other princely patrons, all residing in German territories, are mentioned in the inventories: first and foremost, Friedrich of Württemberg-Teck, who donated several objects ranging from specimens of *terra sigillata* and earth from the Stuttgart area in 1592, to more costly items at a later stage. In the inventory of 1617, there are such

10 KKB, MS GKS, 3467, 8⁰, p. 140: "Steynlyn von den berg Sion bij Jerusalem, dar Christus syn letzte abentmal gehalten hat"; p. 141: "Ein steinlyn oben von den Olijffberg om die gegent dar Christus der Heere nach dem Hemel isz auffgefahren alwar das noch aine von syne fuszstapffen is zu sehn". See also Marika Keblusek, 'Early Modern Grave Robbing. Egyptian Objects in the Collection of Bernardus Paludanus (1550-1633)', in: Pieter ter Keurs, and Holly O'Farrell, (eds), *MCS Yearbook 2021*, Leiden 2022, pp. 89-101.

11 Findlen, *Possessing Nature*, p. 348.

12 The portrait of Paludanus by Hendrick Pot, 1629, is kept in the Frans Hals Museum, Haarlem. Letter from Maurits to Paludanus in Leiden (1596), University Library, PAP 1b.

artificilia like a pearl encased in gold; a silver encased salt cellar made from "coral shells" – red like coral on the outside and white and red on the inside – engraved with the coat of arms of the House of Württemberg-Teck, two "beautiful pyramids of red Egyptian marble" and a beautiful ivory carved "fountain with six calyces with many thorns and flowers on top".[13] Landgrave Moritz of Hesse-Kassel supplied the collection with samples of red, yellow and white earth from the Hesse surroundings, while duke Heinrich Julius of Braunschweig-Wolfenbüttel presented Paludanus with a "beautiful large beaker of German marble, dug up and found by" his father, set on a "heavy and beautiful silver foot".[14] Paludanus must have been held in particularly high esteem by Anna Maria von Anhalt, countess of Liegnitz-Brieg in Silesia, who sent him gifts related to the geological particularities of her territory, like a little cup made from "red Silezian clay" as well as a valuable set of spoons made from jaspis, encased in gold with a ruby on top and other *artificialia*.[15]

The relationship between Paludanus and other donors is less easy to establish. Were these fellow collectors, correspondents and "friends" with whom he exchanged objects or was their connection one of client-patron? Some of his other patrons may be situated in the political realm, and their donations may be interpreted likewise. According to his catalogues, Paludanus received a mummy from Johan Haga, brother of Cornelis Haga, Dutch ambassador in Constantinople. This mummy, he explained in a lengthy note in his 1617-catalogue, had been broken in several parts which then were stuffed in a large trunk – it had been impossible to leave the body intact, since sailors refused to carry bodies on board "for superstitious fear this would bring about storms".[16] Pierre Jeannin, a French diplomat sent by King Henry IV on a mission to the States General in 1607-1609, brought a *Handstein* with a "lovely gold flower grown on top", probably on the occasion of his visit to the Paludanus museum (he also signed the *album amicorum*).[17] A costly gift that can also be construed as official and thus political, came from the Lord Admiralities of the East India Company, the establishment of which Paludanus had been involved in both intellectually and financially (he was a major shareholder). They sent him a:

> beautiful black cabinet made by the Jesuits which our people [*ie* Dutch VOC] have found at sea [*ie* looted], which the Jesuits wanted to bring over to Teru, to put on an altar; in this cabinet are 63 bones of apostles and martyrs and in the middle an *Agnus Dei* with a portrait of Our Lady [*ie* Virgin Mary].[18]

---

13 KKB, MS GKS, 3467, 8⁰, pp. 74; 76-77; 122; 287.

14 KKB, MS GKS, 3467, 8⁰, pp. 233; 288.

15 KKB, MS GKS, 3467, 8⁰, pp. 233; 244.

16 KKB, MS GKS, 3467, 8⁰, pp. 127-128.

17 KKB, MS GKS, 3467, 8⁰, p. 301; KB, MS 133 M 63, fol. 30r.

18 KKB, MS GKS, 3467, 8⁰, p. 129.

Paludanus's close connection with the East India Company as one of its first investors must have been a major factor in the growing number of ethnographic items in his museum from the 1600s onwards. Indeed, a visitor to the collection in 1597 recounted in his travel diary how Paludanus had taken him to the Enkhuizen harbour, where sailors presented him with exotic objects. This happened all the time, Paludanus explained to his guest.[19]

On the other hand, gifts to the Paludanus museum from the Medici' *hortulanus* in Florence, Giuseppe Casabona, or the apothecary Caspar Pantzer from Rostock may be interpreted as a regular aspect of the scholarly system of exchange, which allowed learned collectors to enlarge their collections with materials from elsewhere.[20] Botanists especially made use of their correspondence networks to exchange natural materials, seeds, bulbs and dried flowers. Unlike his friend Carolus Clusius however – who exchanged letters often with things included with his wide network of correspondents – Paludanus rarely mentions this form of object acquisition in his letters.[21] He did gift specimens himself (seeds to Clusius; stones to the great mineralogist Michele Mercati in Rome; antiquities to Ernst Brinck, burgomaster of Harderwijk and an avid collector himself) but whether these were reciprocated remains unclear.[22]

I have found little archival information on purchases Paludanus may have made. In his last inventory, dating to 1624, he uses the Latin phrase *emi* (I have bought) several times, for example in the case of a set of "Chinese paintings" (perhaps scrolls?).[23] But any financial documents that shed light on the amount of money he spent on his museum and that allow for an estimation of the percentage of objects gifted or bought seem not to have been preserved. However, even lacking such financial documentation, it is evident that Paludanus did take good care of his collection and was heavily invested in its maintenance and management. We can conclude this from the way his objects were stored and the way they were described, and of course from the fact that he had his many visitors register their names in his *album amicorum*.

His natural materials and objects were stored in large cabinets, which contained a number of large drawers. Objects that were too large to be contained in drawers were placed on top of the cabinets. These, as we have seen in the visual catalogue of 1592, in turn were divided into little boxes or compartments which could hold an object or

---

19 Frank Boblenz, 'Ein niederländischer Stammbucheintrag des Johann Wilhelm Neumair von Ramsla aus Weimar für Bernardus Paludanus in Enkhuizen von 1597', in: *Weimar-Jena: Die grosse Stadt*, 4 (2011), pp. 262-285, p. 274

20 Rathgeb 1604, not paginated; KKB, MS GKS, 3467, 8⁰, p. 121.

21 On Clusius and his (epistolary) network see Florike Egmond, *The World of Carolus Clusius*, London 2016.

22 Paludanus mentioned these gifts in his letters to Joachim Camerarius, now in the Trew Collection, Erlangen. Letter from Michele Mercati to Paludanus (1580): Leiden, University Library, PAP2.

23 Florence, Biblioteca Laurenziana, Coll. Ashburnham 1828, f. 16v.

a material ("sand from Egypt"). The cabinets were numbered and probably carried a *Titula* or inscription, referring to their contents, which was copied in the various catalogues/inventories and indicated the domain of nature to which the objects belonged. It is probably the reason why Paludanus referred to his "catalogues" as *Indices*: they literally formed the index to his collections – thus conceptually linking the Index and the Museum: the words and the things.

Yet his collection was not a static sort of body of things, slowly growing larger. Part of the management of the museum lay also in the deaccessioning of things. In 1600, Paludanus signed a contract with Landgrave Moritz of Hesse-Kassel, selling an undisclosed number of "*wundersachen*", "wonder things", for the enormous sum of 1500 *Reichtsthaler*.[24] In 1615, he tried to sell off his collection *en bloc*, again to Moritz of Hesse; Paludanus explained in a letter that he was getting on in years (he had turned 65), his heirs were not interested and he was too old to take care of the collection (however, always a collector, he kept on adding things in later years). In his letter to Moritz, Paludanus was adament that the objects in his museum should remain together.[25] Moritz declined, and thus Paludanus sought out other potential buyers – also to no avail. Once one of the most important collections of natural and ethnographic objects around 1600 in Europe, with hundreds of visitors from all over Europe and poetic praise from Hugo Grotius as "a thesaurus of the world, a compendium of everything / The ark of the universe, the depository of sacred", Paludanus's collection fell apart after his death in 1633. In the end nothing came of his ambition to have his museum remain intact.

24 Marburg, Hessisches Staatsarchiv, Urk. 10 nr. 944 (17 June 1600).

25 Letter from Paludanus to Moritz (1600): Leiden, University Library, PAP 2.

Storing and Staging: Baron Edmond's Boxes

Juliet Carey, Senior Curator, Waddesdon Manor

I dedicate this essay to the memory of my mother, Renata Carey (née Hornstein) 1933 – 2012.

This essay is about some beautifully made packing cases at Waddesdon Manor that few visitors to the house get to see but which have fascinated me for years.[1] Based on a curator's experience, it is quite personal and sometimes speculative, but I hope that it will bring these intriguing objects to a wider audience and raise questions about the lives of collected things when they are, supposedly, hidden away. The fabrication of the storage boxes relates them to bookbinding, to cases for instruments and princely treasures and to the history of expertise in the protection and transportation of precious things. Far from being neutral or invisible spaces, these boxes construct new ways of experiencing their contents and making the owner present. They create dramas of enclosure and revelation that encompass erudition and the erotic. For all

1 It began as a paper given at the conference 'Knowledge in a Box: How Mundane Things Shape Knowledge Production', at the Municipal Tobacco Warehouse, Kavala, Greece (26-29 July 2012), which I developed for the Wallace Collection's Seminar in the History of Collecting (27 June 2016). I am grateful to numerous scholars and colleagues whose questions and comments have helped me with research that is still very much in progress, particularly Diana Davis, Caroline van Eck, Jane Finch, Lucy Razzall, Sofia Rodriguez, Christopher Rowell, Tom Stammers, John Whitehead. During the Covid pandemic, the subject caught people's imagination: I am grateful to audiences for their encouraging responses to Zoom lectures, including the Institute of Conservation (26 April 2022) (https://www.youtube.com/watch?v=mcFe_IRcVgc); the boxes featured in a magazine article: Joanna Rossiter, 'The Art of storing and unveiling', *The Spectator*, 24 April 2021.

their aesthetic and tactile appeal, their protective role is underlined by the turbulence of the times that they have survived.

The boxes were made during the 19th century to store, among other things, Sèvres porcelain, small marbles and antiquities.[2] They are still in use at Waddesdon Manor, in England, a National Trust property that houses the Rothschild Collection. During the winter, vases and other works of art are stored in these custom-made boxes and stacked in fireplaces, which are, counterintuitively, the safest places in case of fire or flood. [Figure 6.1]. Some of the Sèvres vases, that are stored in the boxes, can be seen in [Figure 6.2], in their display mode, on the mantelpiece.

Waddesdon Manor was built around 1880 for Baron Ferdinand de Rothschild (1839-1898), a member of the Rothschild banking dynasty, which had its origins in the Frankfurt Ghetto. He was born in Paris, raised in Frankfurt and Vienna and settled in England. The exterior of the house pays homage to French Renaissance châteaux, flamboyant and surprising when first glimpsed on top of a hill in Buckinghamshire. The rooms inside are lined with French 18th-century panelling and stuffed full, with French decorative arts, English, French and Dutch paintings and German *Kunstkammer* objects.

However, the boxes that are the subject of this essay did not originate in England. They were made for Baron Edmond de Rothschild, (1845-1934), a cousin of Waddesdon's Baron Ferdinand. Baron Edmond [Figure 6.3] was part of the French branch of the family and assembled his collections for houses in France, principally 41 rue de Faubourg St Honoré (now the American Embassy) and 29 Avenue du Bois-de-Boulogne (now Avenue Foch) in Paris, the Château Rothschild, Boulogne-Sur-Seine (Hauts-de-Seine) and Château d'Armainvilliers (Seine-et-Marne), and he also used other Rothschild properties at Ferrières and Cannes.

How exactly Baron Edmond moved his collection around is not known but works of art would have been packed away in the boxes when no one was in residence and the house closed up for a season. Baron Ferdinand recalled this pattern of packing and unpacking when he recalled how, in the early 1840s, residing in Frankfurt, his family spent 'the winters in town, and the summer at a villa close by.'

> As soon as the swallows made their appearance my Father's curiosities were packed and stored away in a strong room, where they remained until the cold drove us back again from the country. It was my privilege on these occasions to place some of the smaller articles in their old leather cases, and then again in the winter to assist in unpacking them and rearranging them in their places.[3]

---

2 Most were made in the second half of the 19th century, but some may be from earlier in the century. It is hoped that ongoing research will clarify the dating.

3 Ferdinand de Rothschild, *Reminiscences*, (p. 29 of the paginated typescript, which has manuscript edits and amendments, published in '"Bric-à-brac"' A Rothschild's Memoir of Collecting', ed. Michael Hall, *Apollo* 165, no. 545 (2007), 50-77, 56. Baron Ferdinand remembered that 'merely to touch them sent a thrill of delight through my small frame.'

Baron Edmond's boxes were also used to transport particular works of art between houses, a bit like a medieval king and his tapestries. Boxes at the Villa Ephrussi de Rothschild at Cap Ferrat served that purpose too. Béatrice Ephrussi de Rothschild moved her favourite things around with her, unpacking and installing them as finishing, presence-affirming touches when she arrived. [4]

Baron Edmond's boxes are at Waddesdon because part of his collection was inherited by his son James (Armand Edmond) de Rothschild (1878-1957), who settled in England in the wake of the Dreyfus Affair and inherited Waddesdon from his aunt, Alice de Rothschild. Baron Edmond was arguably the greatest collector in a family of collectors, and his vast collection – much of it now in the Musée du Louvre – has long been the focus of scholarly and curatorial attention. The sociable context of the study and enjoyment of his art is suggested by the numerous chairs and tables in the room in Paris where he kept his prints and drawings, [Figure 6.4] in leather portfolios on shelves, with paintings and sculptures above. However, this essay is not about a collection in use or on display, but about boxes for putting them away.

Baron Edmond's boxes are highly crafted objects. They are pleasing to the eye and to the touch. They are constructed of wood, usually oak, and lined with chamois leather, which is usually red, but sometimes beige. Many of the boxes bear a red leather label lettered in gold. Although many of Baron Edmond's boxes must have been commissioned by him, as they were made for objects that he acquired, it may be that their appearance takes its cue from boxes made for the previous generation.

A particularly large Sèvres pot-pourri vase at Waddesdon [Figure 6.5] – the so-called Copenhagen Vase – was owned by Edmond de Rothschild's father, Baron James Mayer de Rothschild (1792-1868), and its box may have been made for him.[5] As well as cushioning and protecting the vase, the box helps the viewer to study it. The pot-pourri vase is so big that it is difficult to handle and dangerous to turn upside-down, but the box positions it so that one can see the inside of the cover and the marks on the base.

---

4 I am grateful to my colleague Ulrich Leben for sharing this information from his research at the Villa Éphrussi de Rothschild. The storage box for a pink Sèvres porcelain clock is of similar construction to those at Waddesdon. Mia Jackson has recently drawn my attention to and shared correspondence with Viviane Mesqui about boxes at Sèvres Cité de la ceramique (for vases MNC 28435-1&2), previously owned by Guy de Rothschild (1909-2007), whose grandfather, Alphonse James de Rothschild (1827-1905) was the brother of Edmond de Rothschild. It is hoped that further research will clarify to what extent other 19th-century French Rothschilds used storage boxes similar to Baron Edmond's, whether Baron Edmond had more of them than his relations, and whether perhaps he and other Parisian Rothschilds were following a precedent set by his father James Meyer de Rothschild (1792-1868).

5 The 'Copenhagen Vase' is acc. no. 2265. A handful of other works of art at Waddesdon, with a James Mayer de Rothschild provenance, with storage boxes comparable to Baron Edmond's, include a Sèvres ewer and basin (acc. no. 853), the Starhemberg Service (acc. no. 2761) and a Saint Porchaire cup (acc. no. 2773). I am grateful to Mia Jackson for this information.

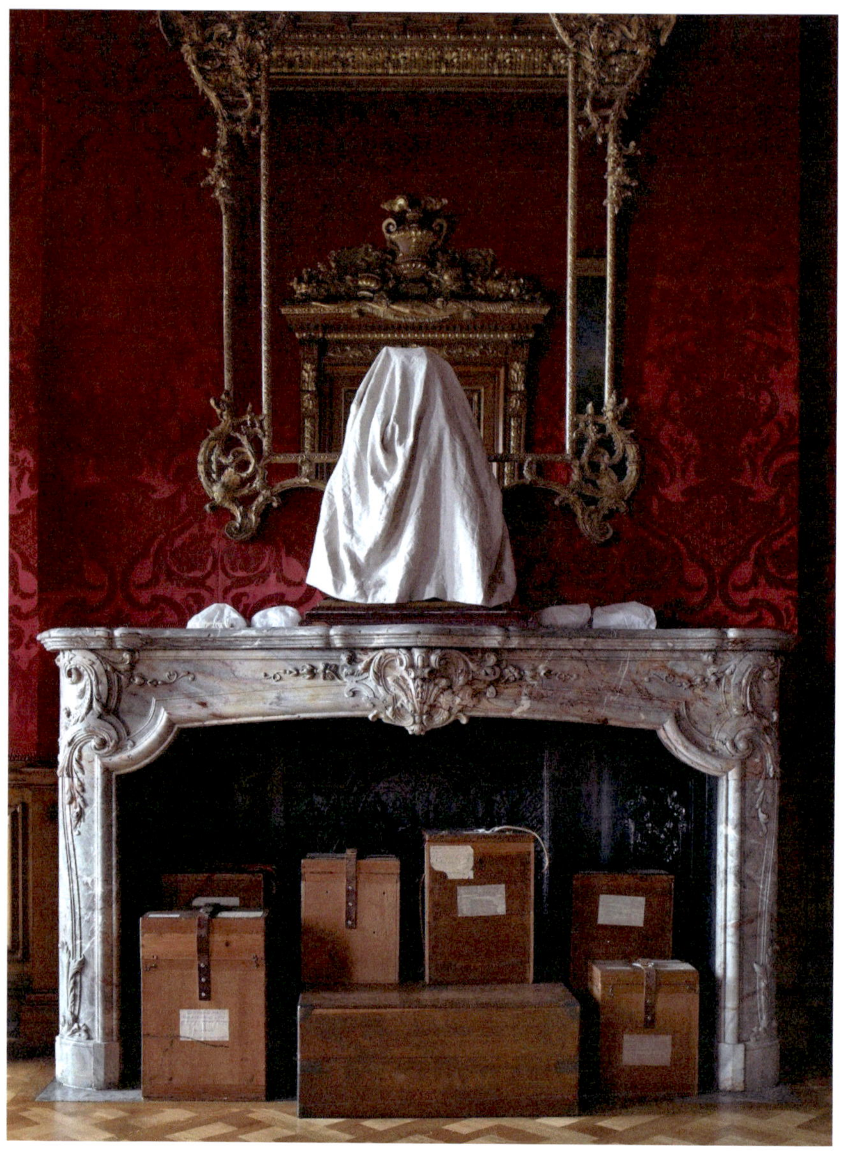

Figure 6.1: Red Drawing Room, Waddesdon Manor during closed season. Photo: Waddesdon Image Library, Paul Baker.

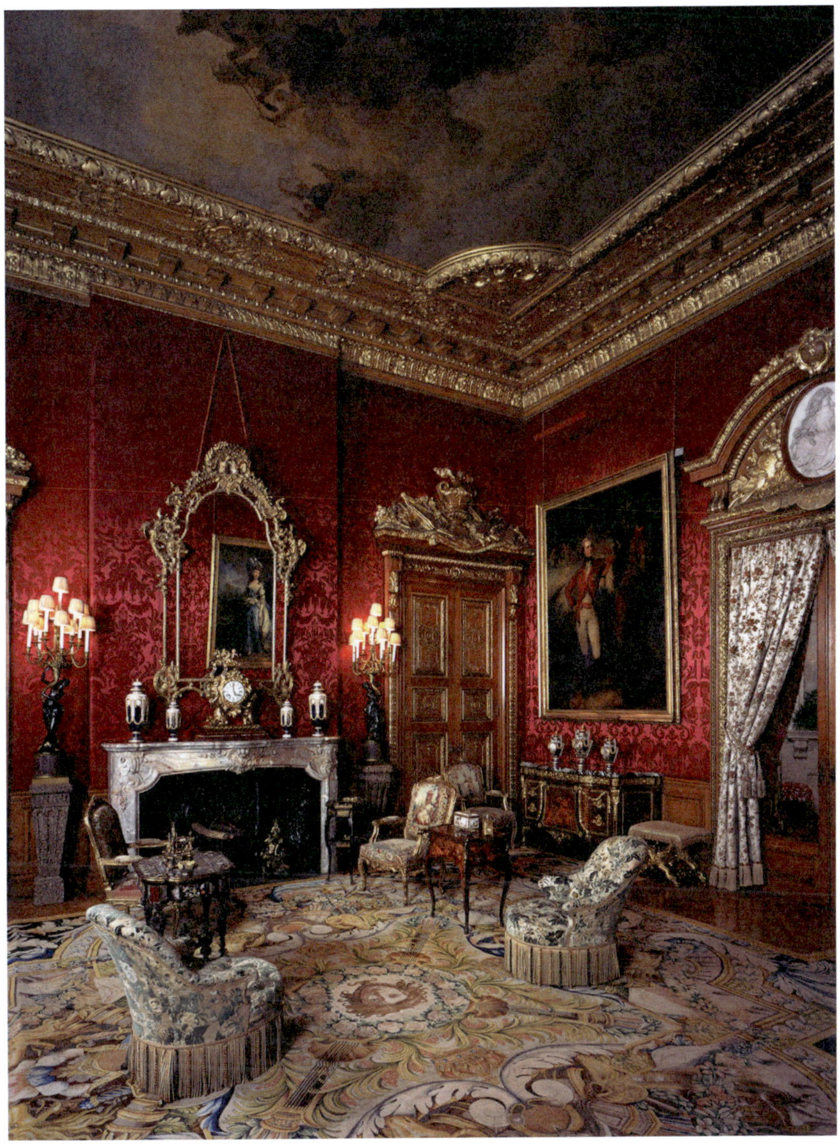

Figure 6.2: Red Drawing Room, Waddesdon Manor. Photo: Waddesdon Image Library, John Bigelow Taylor.

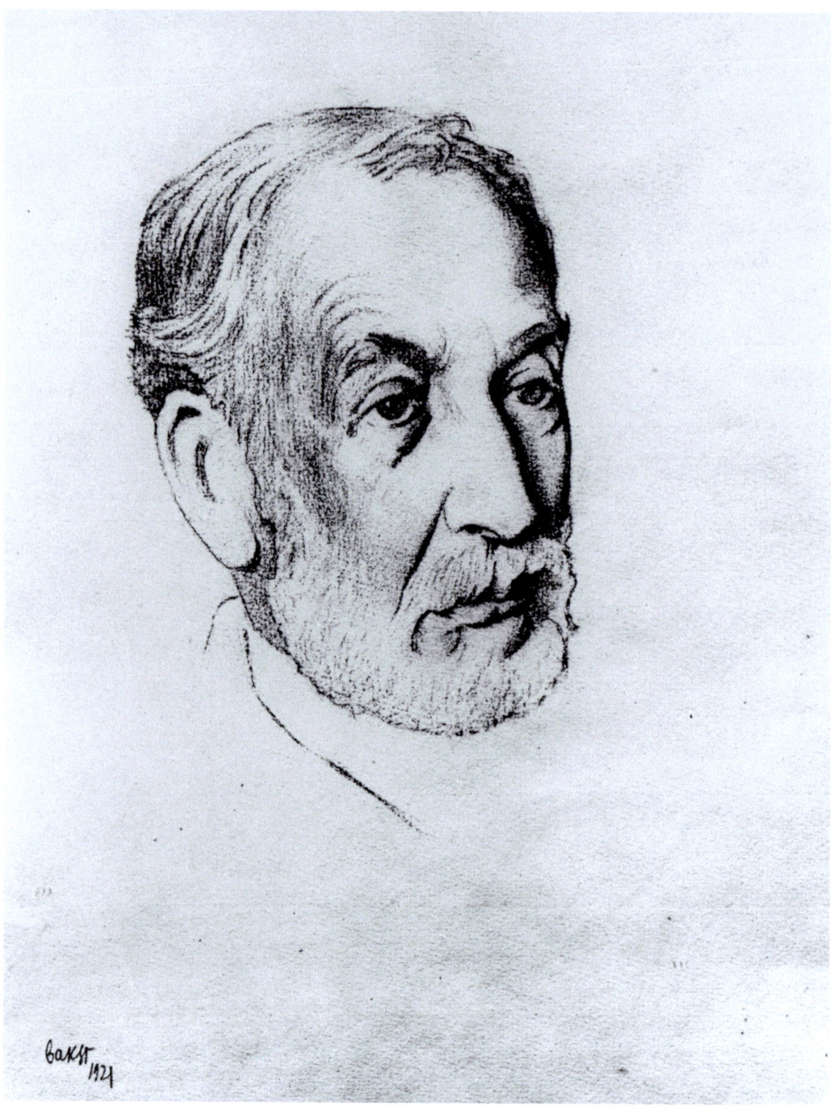

Figure 6.3: Léon Bakst, *Baron Edmond de Rothschild (1845-1934)*, 1921; conté crayon on paper; Waddesdon (Rothschild Family) On loan since 1996; acc. no. 52.1996; Photo: Waddesdon Image Library, Mike Fear.

The materials used in the construction of the storage boxes have uses elsewhere in the lives of the objects they protect. For example, the thin strip of chamois leather added to the lower edge of the cover to protect the edges of the cover and body of the vase from each other when the two parts are put together for display, is the same material as that which covers the conical forms that fit inside the foot of some vases

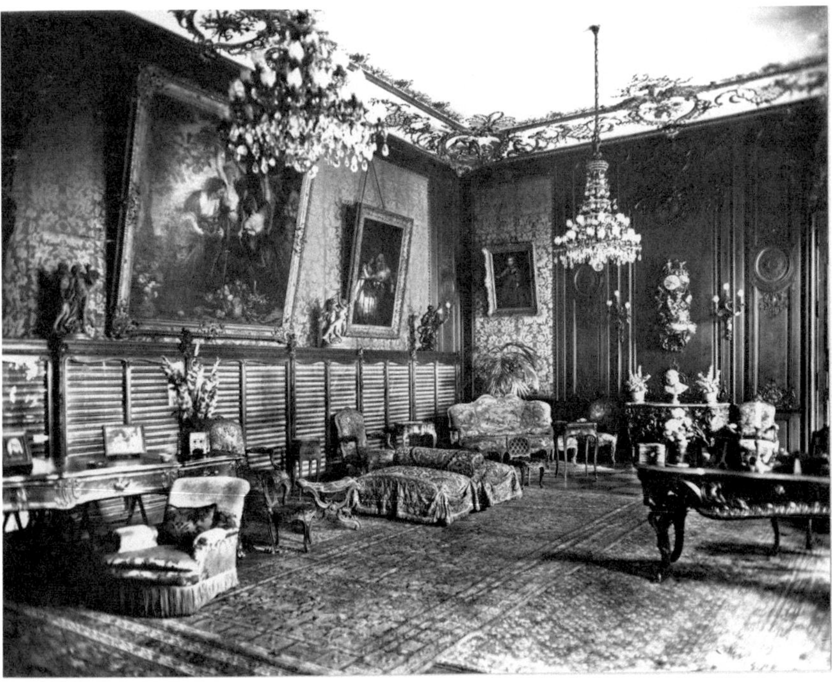

Figure 6.4: The library at 41 rue du faubourg Saint-Honoré Paris, 19th century; Waddesdon (Rothschild Family); acc. no. 155.1997; Photo: Waddesdon Image Library.

to secure them to their display bases.[6] The choice of red chamois for the lining of many of the boxes recalls the dark red velvet that covers numerous stands for small objects at Waddesdon (from both Edmond and Ferdinand), particularly porcelains, at Waddesdon.[7]

It is instructive to compare Edmond's boxes with those of his cousin Ferdinand. Ferdinand owned three Sèvres *vases 'vaisseau à mat*,' among the greatest trophies of all in the world of ceramics collecting but, when they were packed away for the winter, they were stored in much less sophisticated boxes than Edmond's. Ferdinand's boxes [Figure 6.6] do their job, providing a solid shell for the vases, with padded edges to the almond-shaped openings. Shaped planks slot around the vase to keep it stable, but it is always a little unnerving to push these pieces of wood back into place, as though it will chop off the top of the vase. Crude nail holes in the ceiling

---

6 For example, three pink-ground Sèvres vases from Edmond de Rothschild (Waddesdon, acc. nos. 2312, 2314.1-.2.).

7 *Monkey seated on a donkey*, c. 1755, Strasbourg, or perhaps Frankenthal, acc. no. 2425.

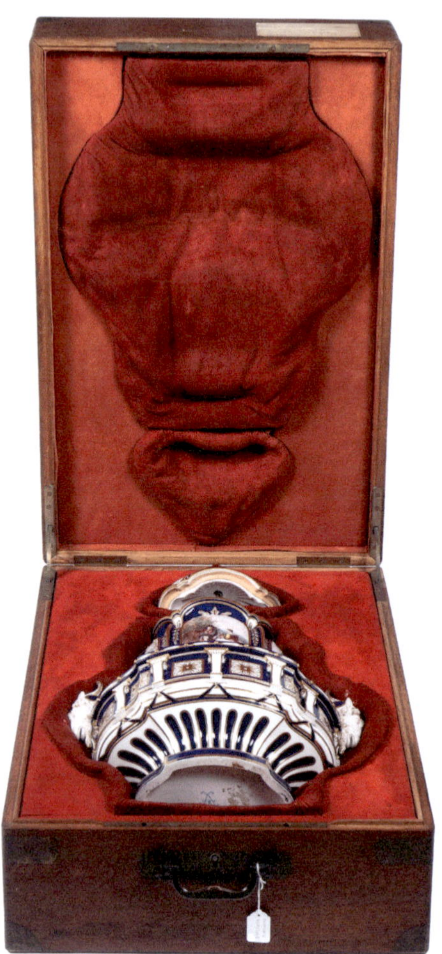
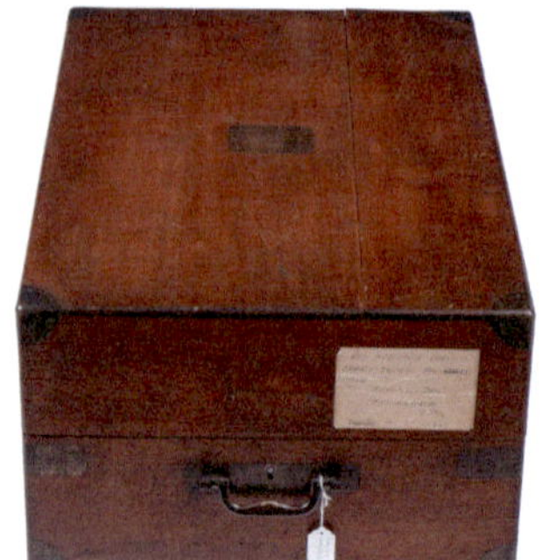
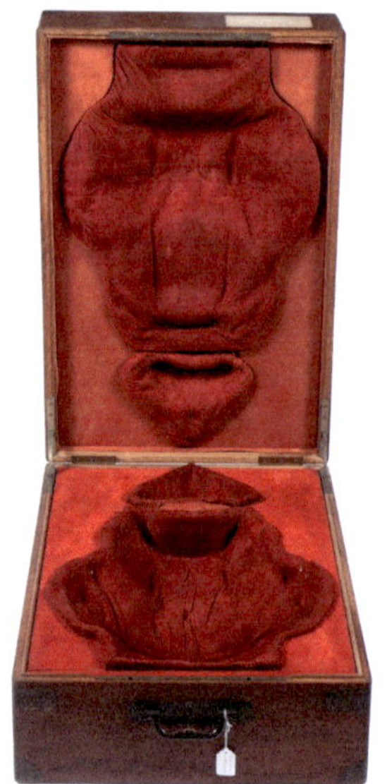

Figure 6.5: Box for the 'Copenhagen Vase'; Waddesdon (National Trust) Bequest of James de Rothschild, 1957; acc. no. 5623; Photo: Waddesdon Image Library, Mike Fear.

of the box show that there were once kidney-shaped pads to cushion the top of the vase but, when closed, the space between the knop of the vase and lid of the box is only a few millimetres.

Baron Edmond's boxes are of another order – with their beautiful corner joins, polished exterior surfaces, flush-fitted brass fixtures and plush interiors. They have something of the robust, reassuring simplicity of strong boxes, such as those seen in the German Jewish painter Moritz Oppenheim's narrative scenes that depict a foundational, if apocryphal, story of the origins of the Rothschild banking firm: Wilhelm I, Elector of Hesse, entrusting Mayer Amschel Rothschild with his treasure when his lands were annexed by Napoleon and retrieving it from his sons after the danger had passed.[8] [Figure 6.7]

The leather labels relate Edmond de Rothschild's storage boxes to the bindings of books and to the tooled leather portfolios and boxes in which he kept his prints and drawings. The animal-skin linings of the boxes recall the long tradition of leather cases for precious objects, including, for example, the covers of scientific instruments, such as the Louis XV microscope in the Getty Museum [Figure 6.8].[9]

Walter Benjamin described the 19th-century Parisian interior as like an upholstered case for a scientific instrument, which seems appropriate to this discussion of upholstered cases made to house works of art in 19th-century Paris. Like 'a shell [which] bears the impression of its occupant', the dwelling encased the person 'with all his appurtenances so deeply in the dwelling's interior that one might be reminded of the inside of a compass case, where the instrument with all its accessories lies embedded in deep, usually violet folds of velvet.' Benjamin continues, encompassing in his sentence the coverings of inanimate objects, spaces, foodstuffs and the human body: 'What didn't the nineteenth century invent some sort of casing for! Pocket watches, slippers, egg cups, thermometers, playing cards – and, in lieu of cases, there were jackets, carpets, wrappers and covers.'[10]

This phenomenon was not unique to the nineteenth century. Baron Edmond's boxes draw on a long evolution of suede- or velvet-lined cases for the protection of precious things. For example, the Green Vault in Dresden has a splendid display of

---

8 Moritz Oppenheim (1800-1882), *Elector of Hesse Entrusting Mayer Amschel Rothschild with his Treasure*, 1859, oil on canvas, Ascott House, Buckinghamshire (National Trust), acc. no. 1535170 [https://www.nationaltrustcollections.org.uk/object/1535170]; the companion work (acc. no. 1535171; https://www.nationaltrustcollections.org.uk/object/1535171) is *Amschel Mayer Rothschild returning the Inventory of the Elector of Hesse who refuses it*. There are several copies of these works, many given as gifts by members of the Rothschild family, including, for example, in the Royal Collection, London (RCIN 421460 and 421110)..

9 Compound microscope and case, c. 1751, Getty Museum, 86.DH.694 [https://www.getty.edu/art/collection/object/103SKQ].

10 *Walter Benjamin, The Arcades Project, translated by Howard Eiland and Kevin McLaughlin prepared on the basis of the German volume edited by Rolf Tiedemann* (Cambridge, Mass. And London, England: The Belknap Press of Harvard University Press, 1999), 220-221.

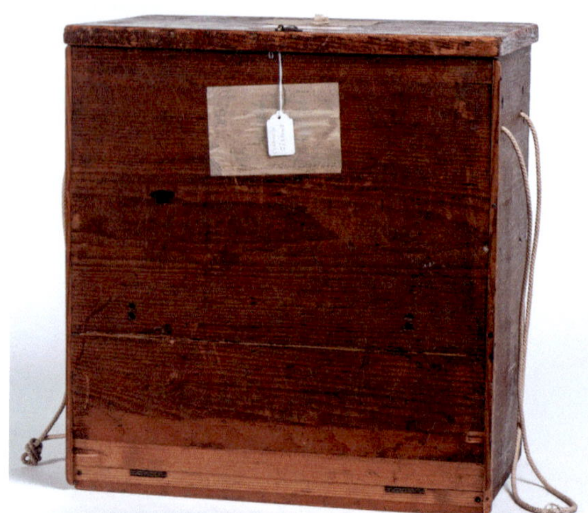

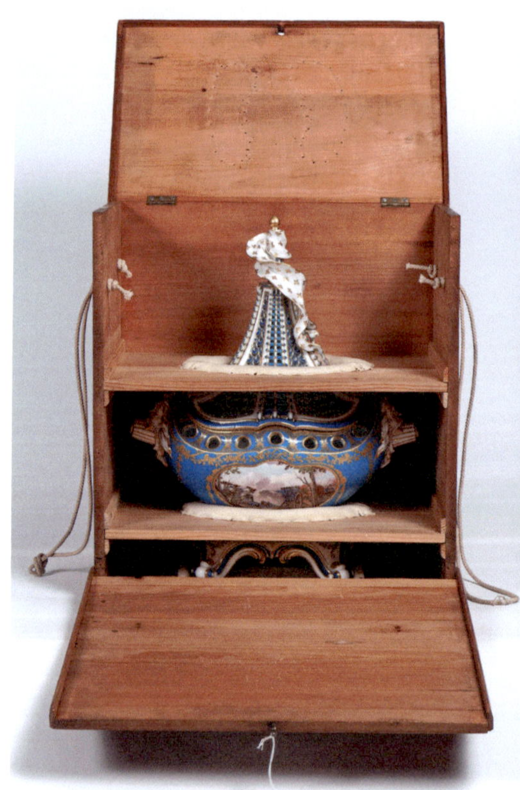

Figure 6.6: Box for a vase *'vaisseau à mat'* (acc. no. 2315); Waddesdon (National Trust) Bequest of James de Rothschild, 1957; acc. no. 5613; Photo: Waddesdon Image Library, Mike Fear.

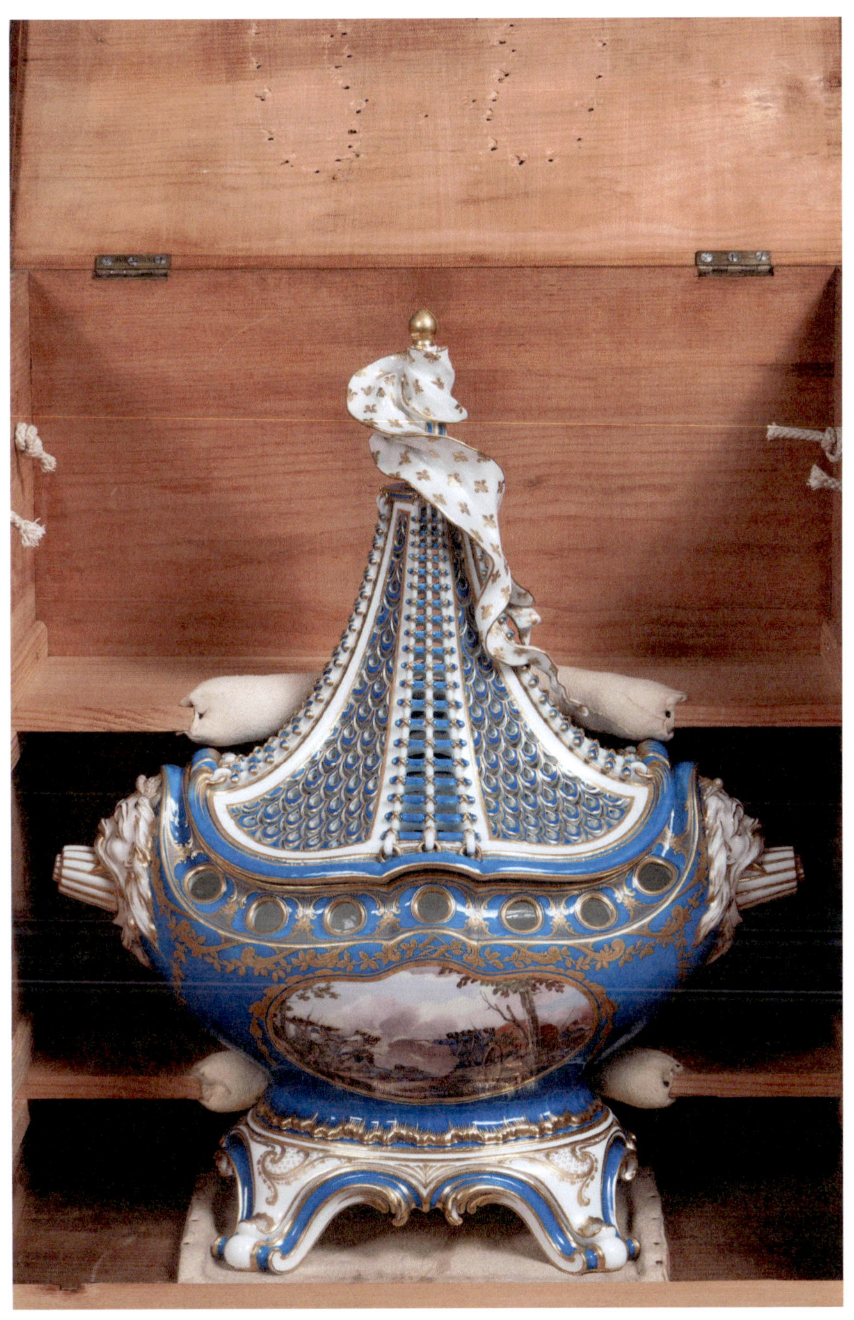

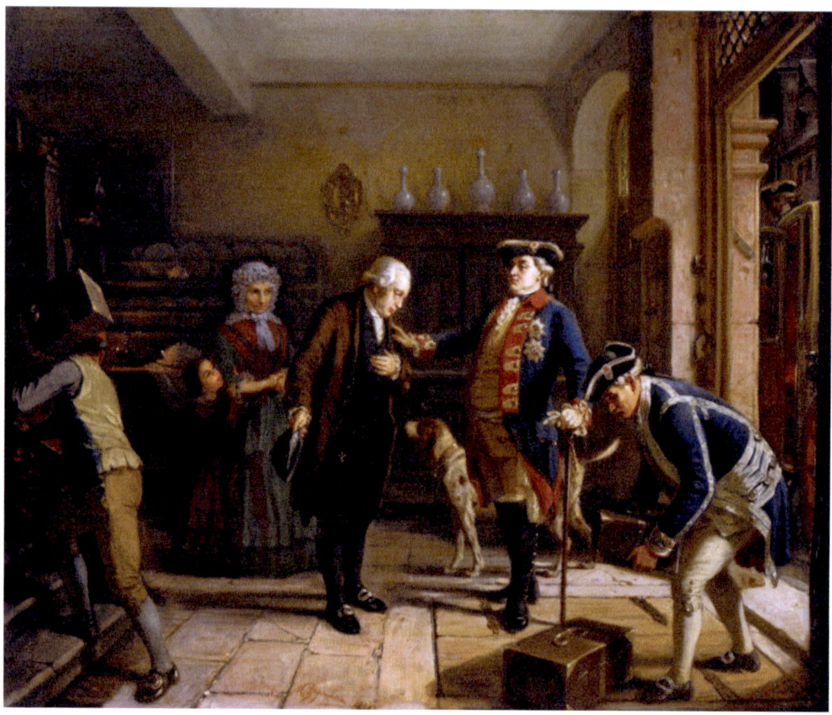

Figure 6.7. Moritz Daniel Oppenheim, *The Elector of Hesse entrusting Mayer Amschel Rothschild (1743-1812) with his Treasure*, 1859; oil on canvas; Ascott Estate, Buckinghamshire; acc. no. 1535170. Ascott © National Trust Images/ John Hammond.

rigid containers for the princely treasures of August the Strong of Poland and Saxony (1670-1733), although the most magnificent collection of such cases – or *étuis* – are in the Prado Museum, Madrid, made for the Treasure of the Grand Dauphin of France (1661-1712). Sometimes with a wooden core, they are made of leather, 'boiled' (heated) for shape and hardness, moulded, stamped and gilded for decoration or covered in brocade or velvet [Figure 6.9-6.10].[11] Allison Stielau has written inspiringly about Renaissance *étuis*, made for the most part by court bookbinders and integral to the presentation of the treasures they housed. She shows how these containers announce their contents as 'objects [that] travel and can be displayed in different

11 The so-called 'Dauphin's Treasure' (Il Tesoro del Delfín), a group of luxury vessels that belonged to Louis, the Grand Dauphin of France and was inherited by his son Philip V (1683-1746), the first Spanish Bourbon, entered the Prado in 1839 and it is now exhibited in its entirety, including the *étuis*. See Letizia Arbeteta Mira, *Il Tesoro del Delfín Catálogo Razonado* (Museo Del Prado, 2001); about the 2018 display, see https://www.museodelprado.es/en/whats-on/multimedia/the-dauphins-treasure/0220d3fc-54eb-1eda-f496-b6f15f370b77.

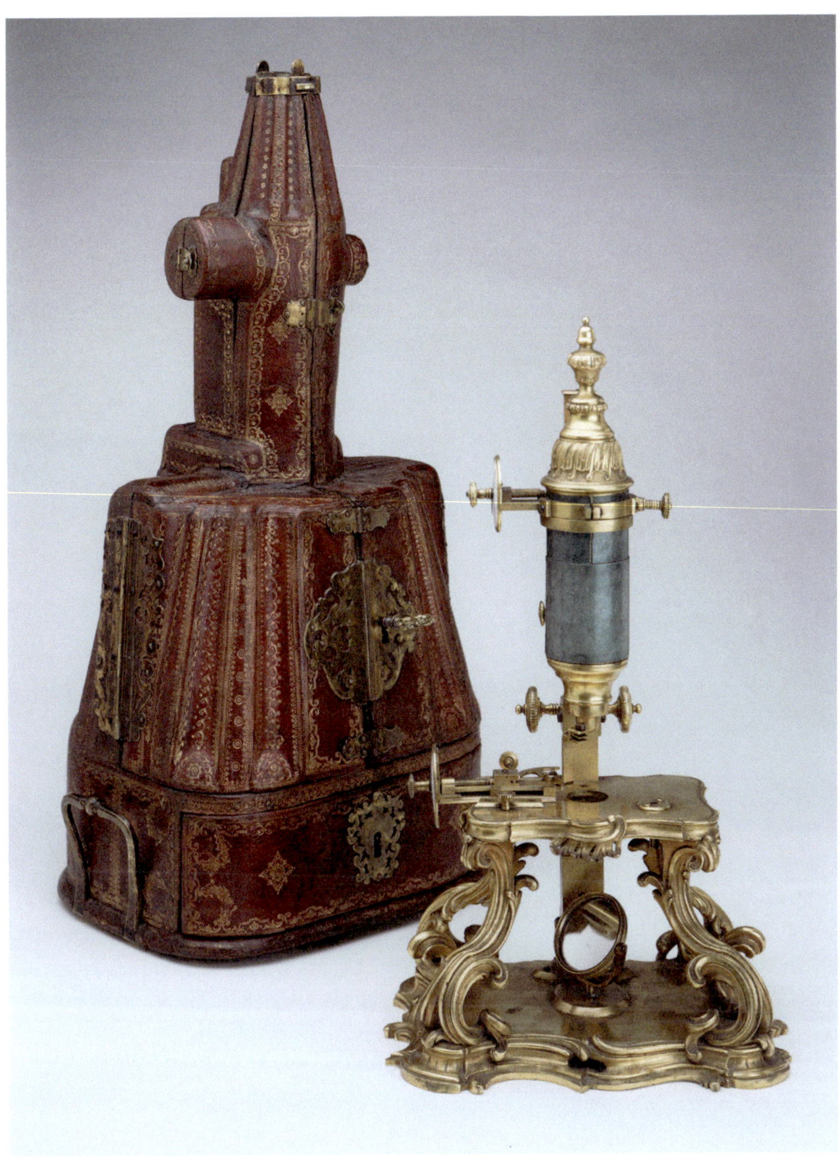

Figure 6.8: Compound Microscope and Case, about 1751; Gilt bronze, enamel, shagreen and glass; wood, tooled leather, brass, velvet, silver galon and various natural specimens; The J. Paul Getty Museum, Los Angeles, 86.DH.694.

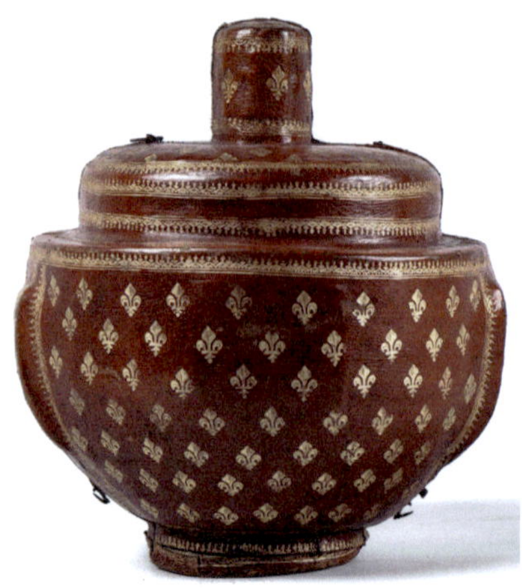
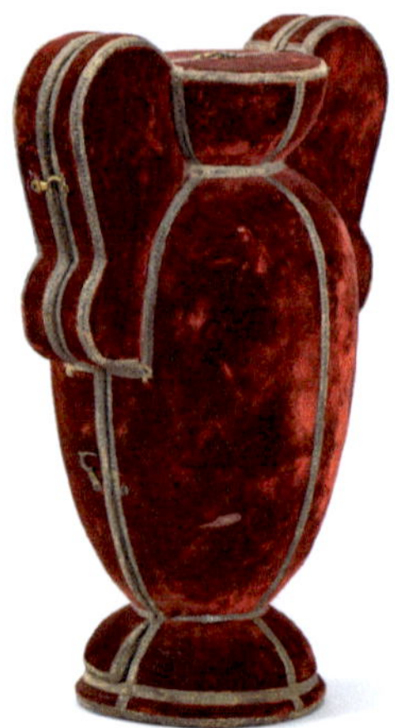

Figure 6.9: Case for rock crystal tazza decorated with stems and a figure of Pallas Athene, early last third of 17th century – 18th century; leather, wood, silk; inv. no. O002963. Case for rock crystal vase with scroll-shaped handles and a decoration of roses, 16th – 17th century; leather, wood, metal, velvet; inv. no. O003046. Copyright ©Museo Nacional del Prado.

locations,' part of a collection that is large enough to need storage and to need identifying marks on the outside of the boxes.[12]

The interiors of these cases are like nests, shaped exactly to receive the object. The ghost-spaces in empty ones reveal the shapes of lost works, like the voids inside Baron Edmond's storage boxes, far more seductively than their modern equivalents in plastozote-lined trays. *Étuis* were laden with significance in their own right and their meanings were mobilised by representation in other works of art. Stielau draws attention to the leather example with carrying straps, being pushed into a sack by a figure just visible on the right-hand side of Martin Shoengauer's *Adoration of the Magi* [Figure 6.11].[13] It is the case for the bulbous vessel being offered to Christ at the same moment, part of the theme of the 'movement of goods and people through space [that] became an increasingly visible marginal subject' in pictures of the Adoration. The inclusion of the container makes the Magi's gifts not only symbolic offerings but also 'crafted vessels, requiring material protection and care.' In other works, empty containers act as *vanitas* symbols, for example, in Holbein's *The Ambassadors*, where the empty lute case contrasts with the case for the wind instrument that still has its pipes inside.[14]

12 Allison Stielau, 'The Case of the Case for Early Modern Objects and Images', *kritische berichte*, 3 (theme of the issue: "Die Kunst und die Dinge. Perspektiven einer schwierigen Beziehung") (2011), 5-16. I am grateful to Sophia Rodriguez for drawing my attention to this publication.

13 Martin Shongauer, *Adoration of the Magi*, c. 1470-75; (https://www.metmuseum.org/art/collection/search/366983); Stielau, op. cit., p. 10.

14 Hans Holbein, the Younger, *The Ambassadors*, 1533, National Gallery, London (https://www.nationalgallery.org.uk/paintings/hans-holbein-the-younger-the-ambassadors); Stielau, op. cit., pp. 13-14.

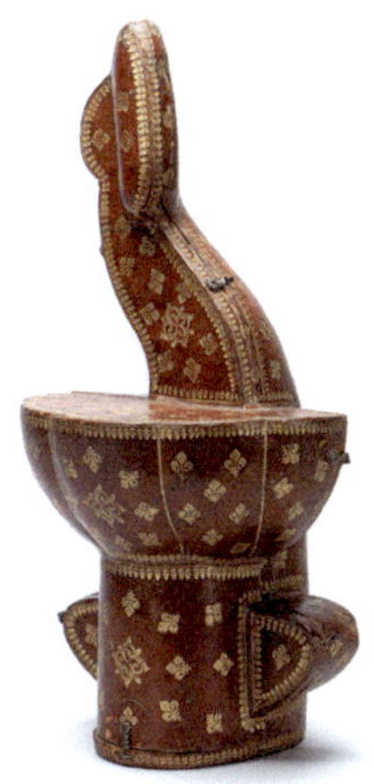

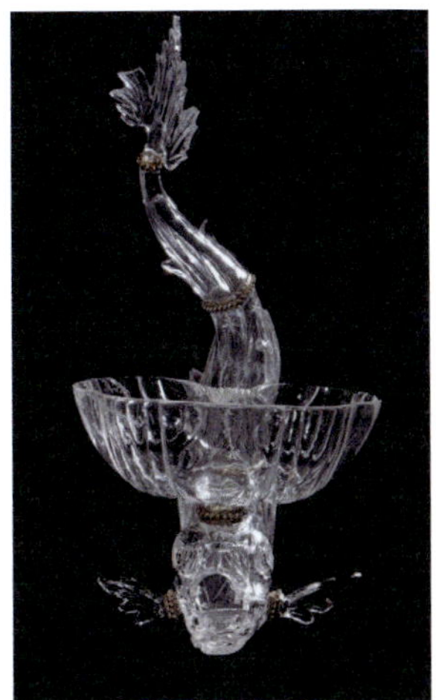

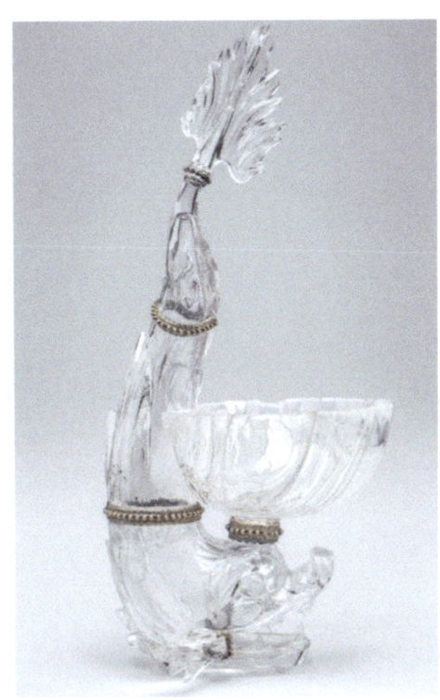

Figure 6.10: Case for rock crystal salt shaker case in the shape of a dolphin, 1670-1711; leather, wood, metal, chamois; inv. no. O003064. Rock crystal salt shaker in the shape of a dolphin, 1670-1711; Rock crystal / hyaline quartz; gold; silver; inv. no. O000113. Copyright ©Museo Nacional del Prado.

Unlike Edmond de Rothschild's boxes, most of the (French-made) containers for the Grand Dauphin's Treasure are embellished with decorative motifs on the outside. Unlike Edmond de Rothschild's rectangular boxes, in most cases the exterior forms of these earlier containers, follow the curves of knops, handles and even a dolphin's tail, hinting at the shape of the object inside. In this, they are more like clothing, fashioned to the body, whereas Baron Edmond's boxes are, from the outside at least, distancing and externalising.[15] However, other aspects of the aesthetics of the *étuis* are shared by Baron Edmond's later, wooden boxes. The fabrication of the box creates anticipation and surprise. The drama of the reveal is central to how they work, part of the staging of the work of art, for the viewer's delight, cushioned in colour.

One example of a Renaissance object complete with its leather case was in Rothschild ownership in the 19th century: a miniature boxwood tabernacle (1500-1530) owned by Ferdinand de Rothschild – part of what he called his 'Renaissance Museum' at Waddesdon, which, at his death, he bequeathed to the British Museum as the Waddesdon Bequest.[16] The opening of the black case, whose exterior is embellished with tooling and gold, and whose interior is lined in red, is a prelude to the drama of the flower-like opening of the many layered, intercessionary object that it houses. A pair of early 16th-century portrait sculptures by Conrad Meit, also in the Waddesdon Bequest, depict Margaret of Austria

15 I am grateful to Caroline van Eck for this insight.

16 Miniature Tabernacle and Case, 1510-1525, British Museum, London, WB 233; http://wb.britishmuseum.org/MCN6655#1509802001

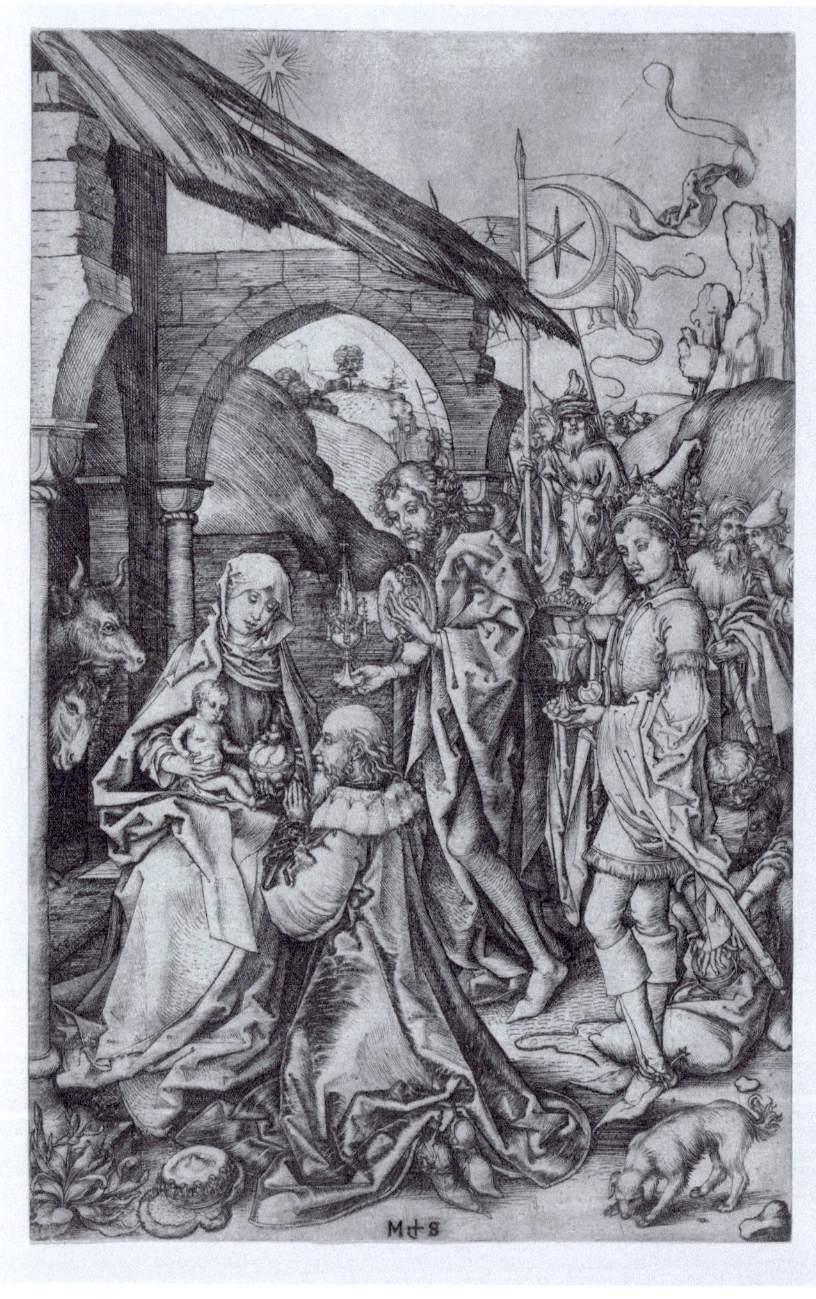

Figure 6.11: Martin Shongauer, The Adoration of the Magi, ca. 1470–1475; engraving; Metropolitan Museum of Art, Harris Brisbane Dick Fund, 1932; acc. no. 32.78.1.

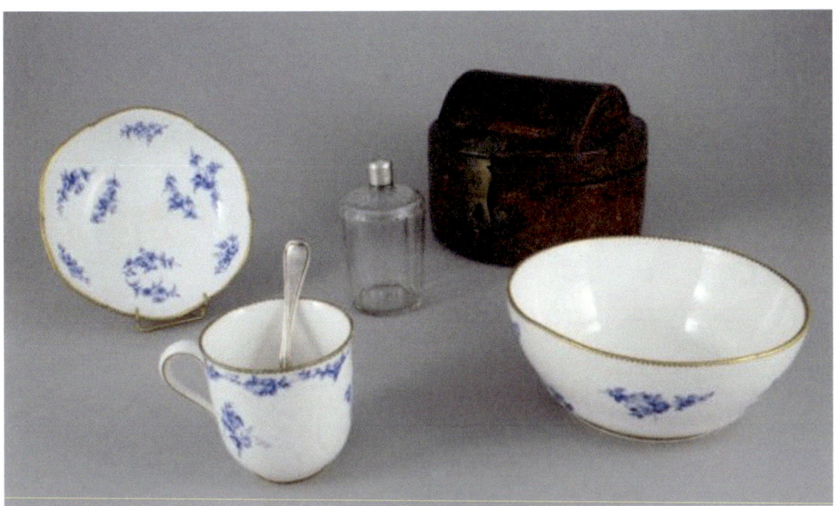

Figure 6.12: Sèvres porcelain manufactory, Cup and saucer (*'gobelet feuille de chou et soucoupe'*) and bowl (*'Jatte Hébert'*), c 1765, with case, courtesy of John Whitehead.

(Regent of the Netherlands) and her husband Philibert of Savoy.[17] They were once owned by the Holy Roman Emperor Rudolf II, who protected their delicate surfaces by keeping them in a wooden box lined with fur.[18]

Examples such as these emphasise the princely traditions implicit in the aesthetics of Baron Edmond's boxes, but the Waddesdon boxes are also embedded in other traditions of packing precious things. For example, they demonstrate continuity with 18th-century Parisian expertise in packaging and transportation, from little travelling cases for tea sets, which challenge the user to imagine how the separate vessels fit inside and alongside one another inside the container [Figure 6.12], to ingenious boxes with a cradle of silk tapes for smoothly raising piled plates.[19]

A box, for the Starhemberg Service [Figure 6.13], which belonged to the Paris Rothschilds, including Baron Edmond, during the 19th century, sorts, protects and shows off the Sèvres porcelain inside. The porcelain was probably bought in Vienna, but the box made in France. It reminds me of letters written by the Duchess

---

17 Conrad Meit, Philibert of Savoy and Margaret of Austria, 1515-25, British Museum, London, WB 261; http://wb.britishmuseum.org/makers/Conrad%20Meit

18 Dora Thornton, *A Rothschild Renaissance Treasures from the Waddesdon Bequest* (London: The British Museum, 2015), 203.

19 The teaset illustrated is in a private collection (thanks to John Whitehead for the photograph); the leather and chamois box (c. 1810) in which Napoleon transported dessert plates from the 'Service des Quartiers généraux' (Sèvres, 1808-10) to St. Helena is at the Château de Malmaison (Inv. M. M. 67.8.1 (don baron Gourgaud, 1967); thanks to Lindsay McNaughton for this information).

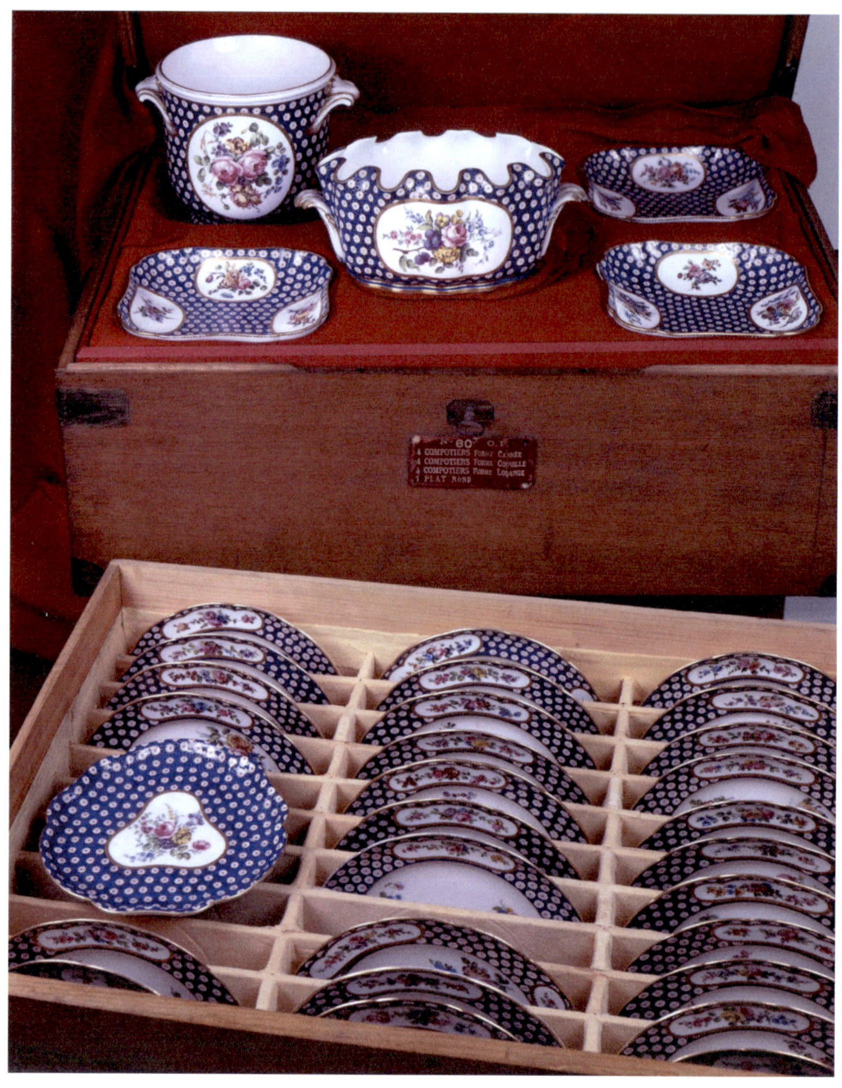

Figure 6.13: Box with part of the Starhemberg Service, Waddesdon (Rothschild Foundation); acc. no. 29.1997. Photo: Waddesdon Image Library.

of Manchester in 1783 fretting about how to safely transport to England the Sèvres dinner and dessert service that had been presented to her by Louis XVI after the Duke of Manchester had helped to negotiate the Treaty of Versailles, which brought about the end of the War of American Independence.[20]

One expense that particularly vexed the duchess, during an expensive year, was having to pay 56 louis 'for the Packing up of my China'. 'I do grudge so much money for Boxes, Paper and Moss', she added. All kinds of materials have been used for the packing of porcelains, including sand, seed husks and peanuts. The marble statues that Thomas Coke, 1st Earl of Leicester brought back from his Grand Tour were packed into wooden crates and held in place with twigs and acorns of evergreen holm oaks, which Coke then planted in his new park at Holkham Hall. But moss was the right material for the Duchess of Manchester's porcelain. She had asked the director at Sèvres to send her someone to pack the porcelain and, she wrote:

> the Man He sent...is the Person employed by everybody as well as by the Manufactory, and is the only one whom he will insure Packing it safe. He cd recommend me another Person who He cd almost be certain wd do so too, but not absolutely sure, & the difference of the Price I find would be only the saving of about 8 Louis or 10 at most, & therefore to run any risk for China of so much value is not worthwhile; So Malgré Moi I must Pay 56 Louis pour l'Emballage.

Such expensive packing was, in itself, a display of wealth and status and when she saw the packer at work she realised why it was so costly:

> the manner the figures are Packed up, is every one in a separate case & the case is made with Hinges – so that all the sides fall down – & shut with clasps – for not a nail is put in, as a knock of a Hammer wd jar the China & Break it all to pieces...

Edmond de Rothschild would have appreciated this eighteenth-century care in packing ceramics. Until recently it was not known who made Baron Edmond's boxes, but colleagues recently found, behind a loose brass number panel, a manufacturer's

---

Carpenters made crates, for the transportation of furniture and objects (see, for example, Trade Card and possible bill-head of Arsandaux, Carpenter, A La Caisse Roialle, engraved by Jeunnié, Waddesdon Manor, 1782, acc. no. 3686.3.18.43; https://waddesdon.org.uk/the-collection/item/?id=16134) but the most refined, leather boxes with fitted interiors were made by members of the guild of *gainiers*, whose depiction in the *Encyclopédie* includes cases for musical instruments and tiny ones for eyeglasses and scissors. For the guilds involved in making different kinds of packing cases see René de Lespinasse *Les métiers et corporations de la ville de Paris*, vol. III, (Tissus, étoffes, vêtement cuirs et peaux, métiers divers) (Paris, Imprimerie Nationale), 1893, p. 482ff.

20 For the Manchester Service (1776-83), in the Royal Collection, see Geoffrey de Bellaigue, *French Porcelain in the Collection of Her Majesty the Queen*, 3 vols (London: Royal Collection Publications, 2009) cat. No. 162, II, 628-659 (the letters are quoted p. 636).

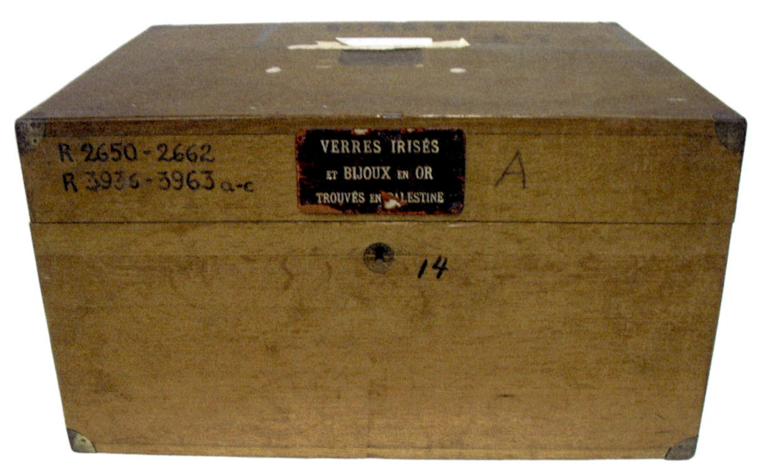
R 2650 - 2662
R 3936 - 3963 a-c
VERRES IRISÉS
ET BIJOUX EN OR
A
14

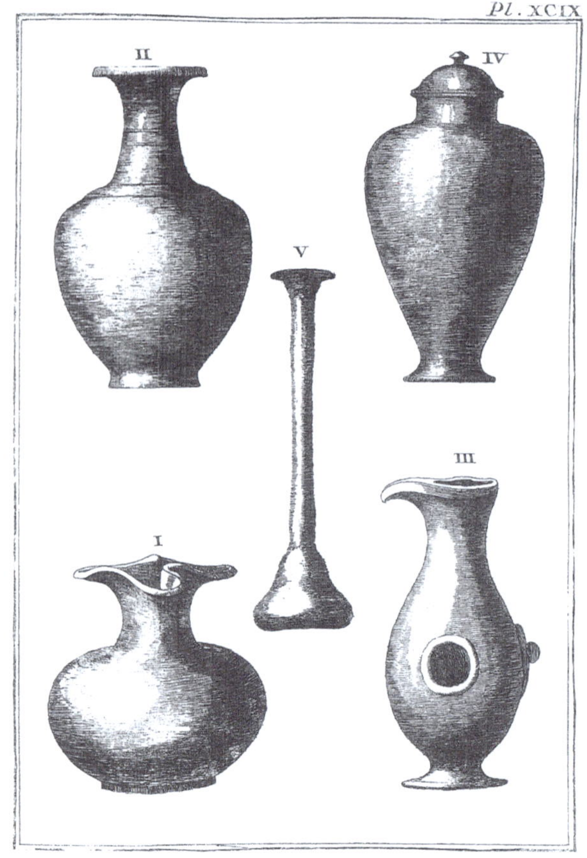
Pl. XCIX
II
IV
V
III
I

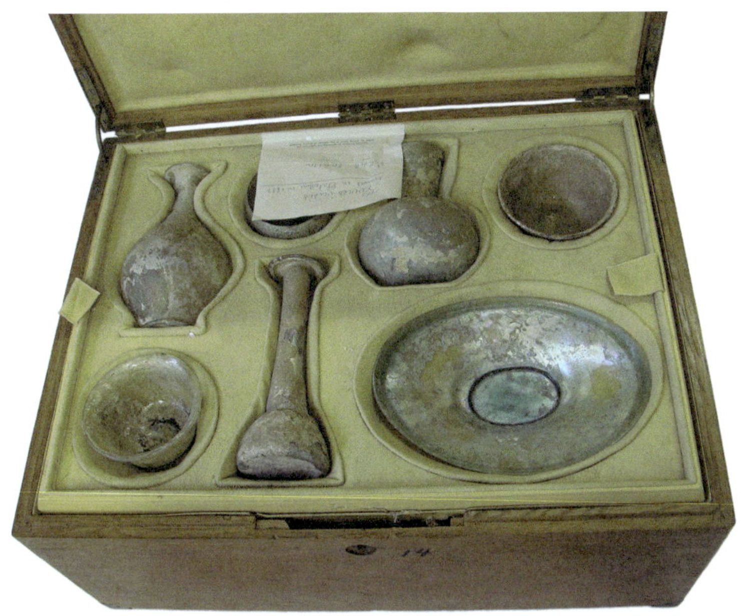

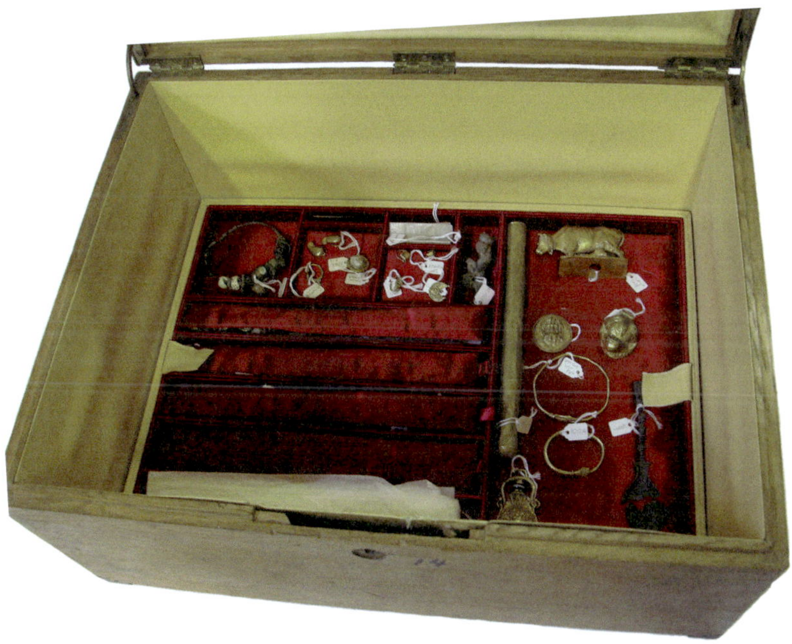

Figure 6.14: Upper left and right: Box with a collection of antiquities; Waddesdon (National Trust). Gift of Dorothy de Rothschild, 1971 aac. no. 8090; Photo: Waddesdon Image Library. Lower left: Anne Claude Philippe, comte de Caylus, *Recueil d'antiquités égyptiennes, étrusques, greques et romaines,* Paris, 1752-67, plate XCIX.

label for Chenue,[21] the *layetier-emballeur*, founded in 1760, which made its name packing Marie-Antoinette's layette (the linen for mother, child and crib) and eventually took on the packing of all the royal linen. It is still the leading company in France for the packing and transporting of works of art.[22]

It is hard to imagine Baron Edmond commissioning any other case makers to make his boxes. He took an intense interest in the packing of his possessions. In June 1882, he wrote to the British consul in Morocco, about the preparation for travel of some faience mosaics that he had acquired for the 'revêtement de deux pièces de mon hôtel.'[23] He wanted each mosaic panel fixed into its own box, with large sheets of paper inside – pressed against each ceramic fragment – so that no single piece would become detached during its journey by ship and wagon. This attention to the relationship between the rigid outside and the softer inside reminds me of the Waddesdon boxes, but on a much larger scale. The Edmond de Rothschild collection at the Louvre provides more evidence of his highly developed interest in the protection of his collection. He left strict rules about the prints and drawings that he left to the museum.[24] He wanted to control how they were kept and handled. According to his instructions, they were to be stored together and to remain separate from other works in the museum, stored in mounts, boxes and shelves whose design he stipulated. In this context, it is interesting that Edmond de Rothschild did not stamp his drawings and prints with a collector's mark, although this was habitual among 19th-century collectors. Might we speculate that Baron Edmond's presence as the owner of his works of art is made concrete in a clear, but non-permanent way, through the enfolding, wrapping and distinctive boxing of objects?

Taking works out of their boxes worried him. People consulting his drawings and prints in the Louvre had to look at them through a sheet of glass. People looking at albums had to do so through a veil of tracing paper – tracing paper, because glass would press too much on the album's spine. Edmond had once turned away a foreign scholar who had come a long way to see his collection because the visitor had a bad cold, so presumably he was particularly worried by the sneezes of the future public at the Louvre.[25]

---

21 Thanks to Jane Finch and Mia Jackson for this discovery – the box is for the ewer and basin inherited from by Edmond from his father [acc. no. 853] although it is not yet known if the box was commissioned by father or son.

22 See Yves Lemoine and Jean-Charles Le Roux, *Chenue A Layetier-Emballeur for 250 years* (Paris: Michel de Maule, 2010). I am grateful to Federico Aimaro and Christophe Piette at Chenue for their search for information about the commissioning of Edmond de Rothschild's boxes which it is hoped will yet bear fruit.

23 Elizabeth Antébi, *L'homme qui racheta la terre sainte* (Monaco : Éditions du Rocher, 2003), 83.

24 Thanks to Séverine Lepape and Victoria Fernandez for this information and for sending me a copy of the typed list of conditions on which his donation of works of art depended.

25 Antébi, op. cit, 85.

In her biography of Edmond de Rothschild, Élizabeth Antébi described the prints and drawings – that were the heart of his collection – as part of the culture of the *flâneur* rather than the culture of display: far from ostentation and market speculation, they were about private enjoyment, shared with a small group of initiates, about enjoyment of beauty and fear of death.[26] Baron Edmond said that he feared completing his collection and he feared completing its setting. He said: 'Tant que la maison n'est pas finie, la mort ne vient pas!'[27] Antébi links Edmond's collecting – his obsession with authenticity and quality and his powerful sense of the precariousness of his collection – with his spirituality. I wonder if his preoccupation with the practicalities of boxing, transporting and protecting his collection can be added to this. Each box makes of a work of art something precious that can be displayed with great brilliance, but that also has an existence – an aesthetically pleasing existence – cushioned and revered in a box.

There is not always a simple split between display and storage – exposing an object for display and placing it in a box, out of sight. Living with my teenage daughter over the Covid pandemic lockdowns intensified my awareness of the drama of the boxing and the unboxing of things. Lydia introduced me to the weird phenomenon of 'unboxing' videos – of shoes, iPhones, all kinds of desirable material goods. Un-boxing is a drama that relies on the significance of the boxing-up in the first place. Boxing something can, paradoxically, show it off, perpetuate information about its provenance, and make visible its value. The Japanese tradition of the *tomobako* is interesting here. Made to house particularly prized porcelain wares; made of special wood, often from a special tree (Paulowania), these boxes were often inscribed with the name of their owner and, more recently, with the name of the maker. The box – and opening the box to reveal what is inside – adds meaning to the object inside. Sometimes, in modern examples, a plastic covering on the lid highlights the value placed on the box itself, the plastic protecting the inscriptions on the lid. Traditions have developed around the closing of the box too, not least in the way a textile tape is tied around the outside. Like Baron Edmond's boxes, they can have textile cushioning inside the base. Some are wrapped in cloth as well as tied with tape and this covering of something precious to express reverence is also reminiscent of religious practices, not least the way the Torah scrolls are kept hidden and safe with a combination of rigid housing and textile covering, like the Torah scrolls boxed and textile-covered on the altar table of the La Grande Synagogue de la Victoire in Paris ('the Rothschild synagogue', built in 1874).

26 Antébi, op. cit., p. 85.

27 [as long as the house is not finished, death cannot come], Suzanne Coblentz, *La Collection d'estampes Edmond de Rothschild au musée du Louvre* (Paris: Éditions des Musées Nationaux, 1954), 22 (quoted Antébi, op. cit., p. 85).

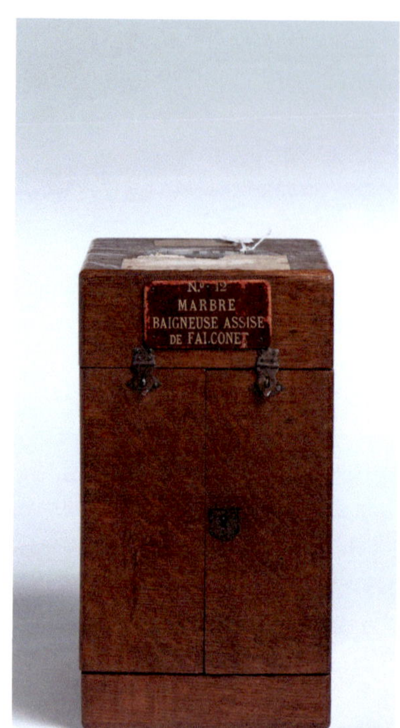

Figure 6.15: Box for *Seated Nymph*, attr. Étienne-Maurice Falconet (acc. no. 2297); Waddesdon (National Trust) Bequest of James de Rothschild, 1957; acc. no. 5615; Photo: Waddesdon Image Library, Mike Fear.

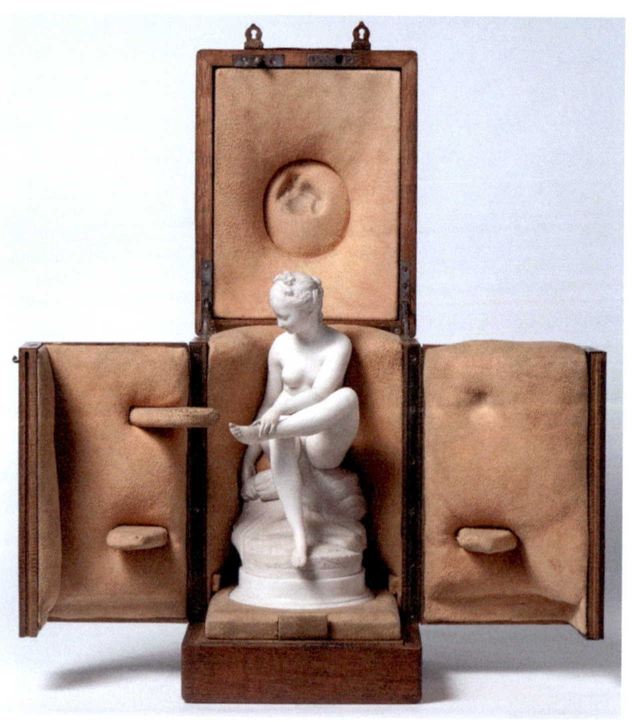

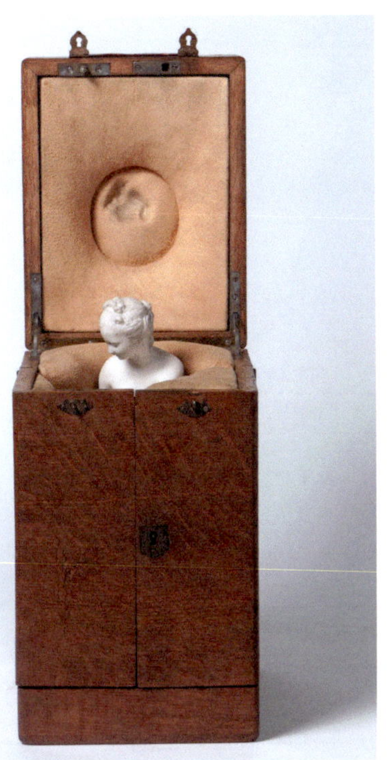

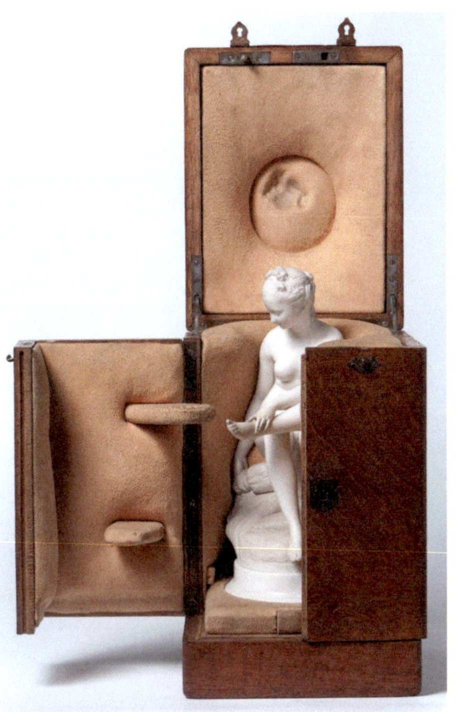

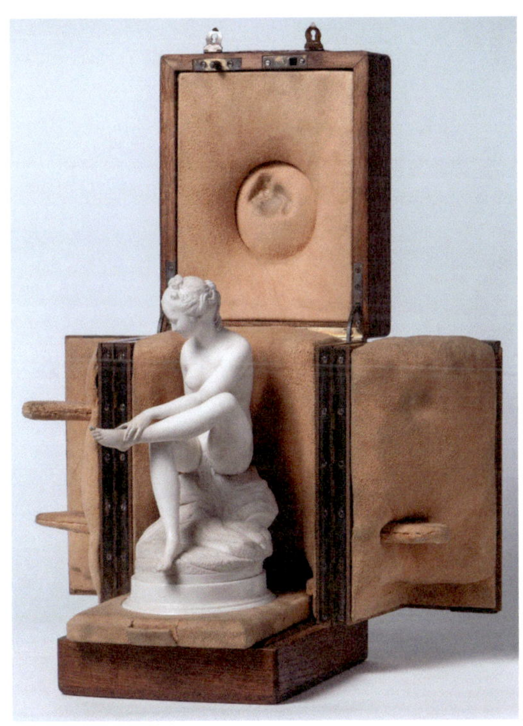

Baron Edmond's boxes at Waddesdon certainly protect their contents, but they also function as frameworks for display and place works of art in visual contexts that range from the scholarly to the erotic. One of the boxes at Waddesdon was made to contain antiquities found in Palestine (Baron Edmond funded many archaeological expeditions) [Figure 6.14]. The box has layers – to store, but also to present to the viewer – different objects in different ways. The lining is predominantly sandy coloured, but the very bottom layer is lined in red silk – with little compartments like a jewellery box. This change in colour is carefully considered, because small, mainly gold objects are stored there, some of which is jewellery. The two trays above are covered in beige chamois – and contain Roman glass vessels. The arrangement of Roman glass on the uppermost layer resembles didactic illustrations in books on antiquities, such as plates in the comte de Caylus's *Recueil d'antiquités*, a founding example of that tradition.[28]

Three boxes much larger than all the others, lined in wool and with double doors that open outwards, have been found in store at Waddesdon.[29] Their labels show that they were made to house furniture.[30] All three were made for furniture inlaid with Sèvres porcelain plaques. [31] Other examples of Baron Edmond boxing furniture in this manner may yet be found (and there is a long tradition of valuable furniture being sold with and transported in specially made cases),[32] but, if these three examples are as unusual as they appear, it reveals something about how he categorised these objects: with his Sèvres porcelain, rather than with other examples of French cabinetmaking.

The most elaborate of the boxes (and my favourite, although curators are not supposed to have favourites) houses a marble nymph attributed to Falconet.[33] It creates a drama of enclosure and exposure, hiding and revealing. [Figure 6.15] First, the lid opens; then one wing opens; then the other. Instead of the figure sitting in a depression inside the base, the box gives the sculpture a little internal plinth, which, with the double doors, makes it like a secular triptych or profane shrine. One pulls the sculpture towards one by pulling a tab on the front of the stage-like platform. The concavities in the padded lining combine practicality with sensuality. The more time the nymph spends in the box, the more precisely the dimples in the padding match

---

28 Anne Claude Philippe, comte de Caylus, *Recueil d'antiquités égyptiennes, étrusques, greques et romaines*, Paris, 1752-67, plate XCIX.

29 Thanks to Jane Finch and Matthew Waters.

30 For example, one red leather label bears the gilded lettering: No 4/BUREAU L. XV/BOIS 17 PLAQUES SÉVRES [sic].

31 Martin Carlin, writing tables: c. 1770, acc. no. 2334; c. 1766, acc .no. 2336; attr. Martin Carlin, Candlestand, c. 1774-c. 1776, acc. no. 2283.)

32 Olivia Fryman gave a talk 'Trunks, Cases and Cabinets for Royal Furnishings and Household Goods', at the National Trust conference 'The Art of the Box', Waddesdon Manor, 3 October 2017.

33 Attr. Étienne-Maurice Falconet, *Seated Nymph*, acc. no. 2297.

her contours. In this particular box, the chamois chosen for the lining seems flesh-coloured – warm, soft and giving, against the marble.

For all their sensory appeal, the history of Baron Edmond's boxes underlines the protection they have given to their contents through time.

They are solid, functional boxes. They have accrued new labels as they have moved around, not always as elegant as the original leather or brass ones, adapting them for use in different storage settings. They have safeguarded their contents through very real dangers. And dark times indeed. In an unfinished memoir, Baron Edmond cites events during the 1848 Revolution as some of his earliest memories. He was not yet 3:

> Mes premiers souvenirs datent du coup d'État de Napoléon III. Mes souvenirs me reportent à cette époque et je vois encore toutes les bonnes de la maison affolées dans ma nursery en entendant la fusillade sur le boulevard…[34]

He remembered how, during his lifetime, 'l'histoire de la terreur […] restait encore dans les esprits au souvenir des horreur de la Révolution française.[35] During the Siege of Paris by the Prussians in 1870-71 Edmond was 26 and a soldier in the Garde Mobile. He wrote that 'Je ne veux pas décrire le siège de Paris' and does not go into any detail about what he called 'toutes les duretés de cet hiver, terrible et glacial.' He talks about eating elephant and kangaroo from the zoo but keeps an emotional distance in his account by concentrating on military, political and economic narratives of the Siege and the Commune that followed it. There is much more research to be done into Edmond's experiences in and around Paris at this time, and of desperate violence much further afield and in subsequent decades – his life and philanthropic activity was transformed by news of the pogroms in Russia – but one might speculate that these experiences affected his perception of danger to his collection and the way he cared for it. In this area, which I want to research further, two verbal descriptions of the boxing up of works of art during the Siege of Paris stick in the mind – not Baron Edmond's descriptions, but from the *Journal* of the collector, writer and publisher Edmond de Goncourt, who wrote on the 3rd of September 1870: 'Ce n'est pas vivre, que de vivre dans ce grand et effrayant inconnu, qui vous entoure et vous étreint'[36]

---

34 [my first memories date from the time of Napoleon III's *coup d'état*. Looking back, I can still see all the panic-stricken housemaids in my nursery when they heard the shots in the street] Edmond de Rothschild, *'coup d'œil sur ma jeunesse par un octogénaire'*, unpublished typescript c. 1930. ERX2/2/18/4 private collection, The Waddesdon Archive at Windmill Hill.

35 [the history of the terror… remained in people's minds at the thought of the horrors of the French Revolution; [I do not want to describe the Siege of Paris]; [the privations and hardships of that terrible, icy winter.] Edmond de Rothschild, op. cit.

36 [It is not life to go on living in this great and terrifying unknown, which surrounds you and crushes you.] Edmond et Jules de Goncourt *Journal Mémoires de la vie littéraire. Édition Définitif publiée sous la direction de l'Académie Goncourt* (Paris: Ernst Flammarion and Fasquelle, 1935), 4 vols, vol. IV, 17.

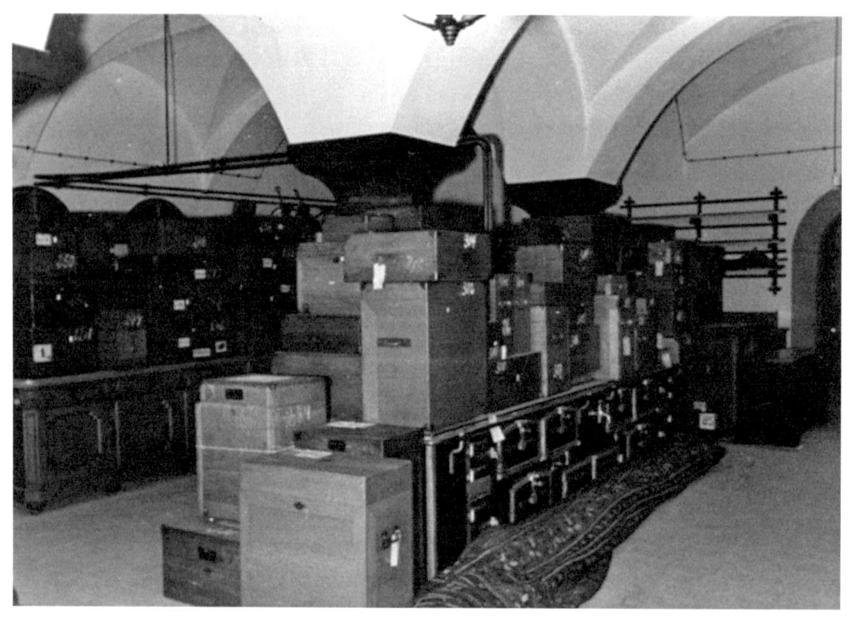

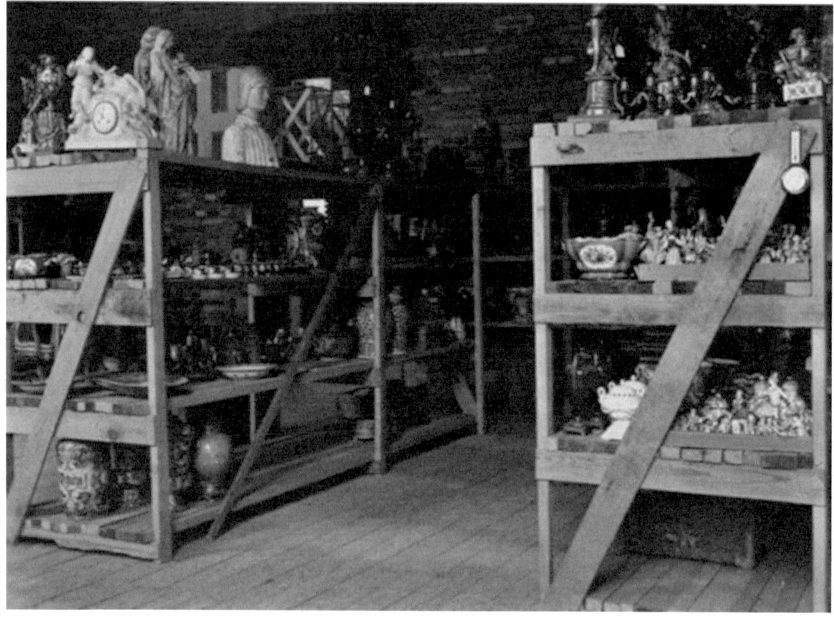

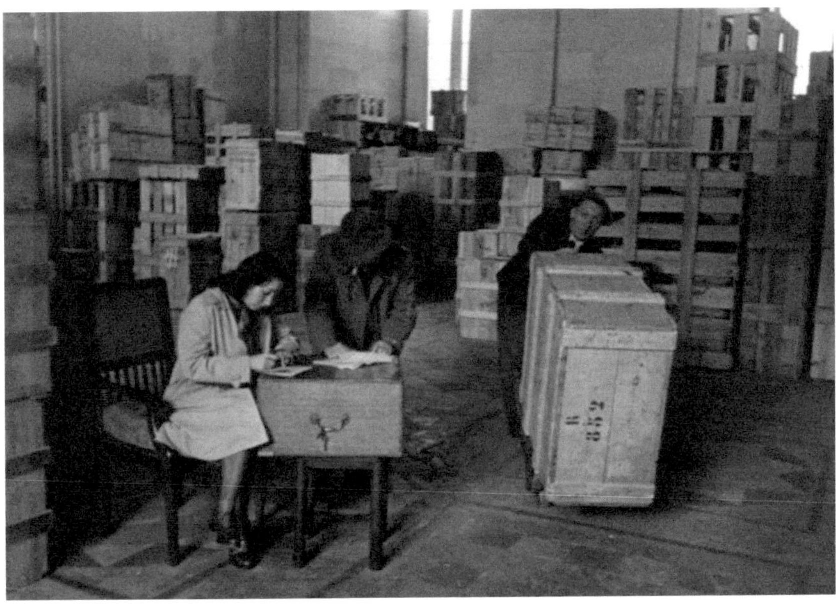

Figure 6.16 (opposite page and above): ERR depot of Neuschwanstein, Germany—chests from the Rothschild collection containing busts, porcelain, crystal and other works. — Bundesarchiv, B323/310; ERR depot of Neuschwanstein, Germany—Miscellaneous works, including clocks (from the Levy-Hermanos collection), Chinese 18th-century majolica vases (from the Stern collection), late 15th-century Italian bust (foreground) from the Seligmann collection. — Bundesarchiv, B323/310. Processing of looted cultural property in one of the M-Aktion camps (either Austerlitz or Bassano). In foreground, a worker moves crate R 852 containing items from the Rothschild family. — Bundesarchiv, B323/311.

The previous day, Goncourt had caught hold of the curator, Charles-Philippe de Chennevières, coming out of the Louvre, who told him he was going to Brest to escort a consignment of pictures – taken out of their frames and rolled up – to save them from the Prussians.[37] Chennevières described 'le triste et humiliant spectacle de cet emballage' and another curator ' pleurant à chaudes larmes, devant « La Belle Jardinière » au fond de sa caisse, ainsi que devant un mort chéri, tout près d'être cloué dans le cerceuil [sic].[38]

---

37 Goncourt, op. cit., pp. 16-17. J'accroche, en sortir du Louvre, Chennevières qui me dit partir demain pour Brest, afin d'escorter le troisième convoi des tableaux du Louvre, qu'on a enlevés des cadres, qu'on a roulés, et qu'on envoie, pour les sauver des Prussiens, dans l'arsenal ou le bagne de Brest. Il me peint le triste et humiliant spectacle de cet emballage.]

38 Goncourt, op. cit., pp. 16-17 [the sad and humiliating spectacle of this packing' and another curator 'weeping hot tears before [Raphael's] "La Belle Jardinière" at the bottom of her packing-case, as if she were a dead friend, ready to be nailed up in her coffin.']

In the evening Goncourt saw outside a railway station:

> les dix-sept caisses, contenant l'Antiope, les plus beaux Vénetiens, etc.; – ces tableaux qui se croyaient attachés aux murs du Louvre pour l'éternité, et qui ne sont plus que des colis, protégés seulement contre les aventures de déplacement, par le mot : *Fragile.*[39]

If the traumatic experience of his own times heightened Baron Edmond's sense of the vulnerability of life and objects, for his collection, the worst danger came a few years after his death (he died in 1934). During the Second World War, the Nazis took much of his collection from his heirs. Many of the boxes at Waddesdon still bear the black identification numbers of the ERR (Eensatzstab Reichsleiter Rosenberg), the taskforce responsible for the plunder of cultural property from Jews and other 'enemies' of the Third Reich. There are photographs showing some of the Rothschild boxes stacked in a Paris depot [Figure 6.16] Their robustness can be compared to the more vulnerable, unboxed works from other big Paris Jewish collections on adjacent shelves. One of the boxes serves as a writing desk for a clerk making notes.

Seeing images of Baron Edmond's boxes, one furniture historian was reminded of a description of Stefan Zweig's visit to an exhibition of furniture with the German-Jewish writer Otto Zarek. Looking at some giant medieval chests, Zweig asked 'Can you tell me which of these chests belonged to Jews'. Zarek was baffled as there were no obvious marks of ownership on any of them, but Zweig smiled. "Do you see these two here? They are mounted on wheels. *They* belonged to Jews...Yes, these chests on wheels are striking symbols of the Jewish fate."[40] The meticulousness of Nazi records allow one to follow the looting, recording and transportation of the Rothschild boxes to the gathering place in the Jeu de Paume and thence to various depots, including the so-called Lager Peter in the Altaussee salt mines in Austria.[41] These are among the precarious journeys invoked in an installation about objects, vitrines and boxes – about storing and staging – that Edmund de Waal's made in response to the sight of the storage boxes stacked up in the fireplace (*on the properties of fire*, 2012)

---

39 Goncourt, op. cit., p. 17 [the seventeen cases, containing the Antiope, the finest Venetians, etc. those pictures which believed they were to hang on the walls of the Louvre for all eternity, and which are now mere luggage, protected against the accidents of removal only by the word "Fragile"]

40 I am grateful to Matthew Benjamin for giving me this reference in response to a version of this essay given as a Zoom lecture to the Furniture History Society, 1 November, 2021; quoted in George Prochnik, *The Impossible Exile: Stefan Zweig at the End of the World* (London: Granta, 2015), 141. The missing part of the quotation is 'In those days indeed always! – the Jewish people were never sure when the whistle would blow, when the rattles of pogrom would creak. They had to be ready to flee at a moment's notice...]'.

41 Cultural Plunder by the Einsatzstab Reichsleiter Rosenberg, https://www.errproject.org, accessed 23 June 2023.

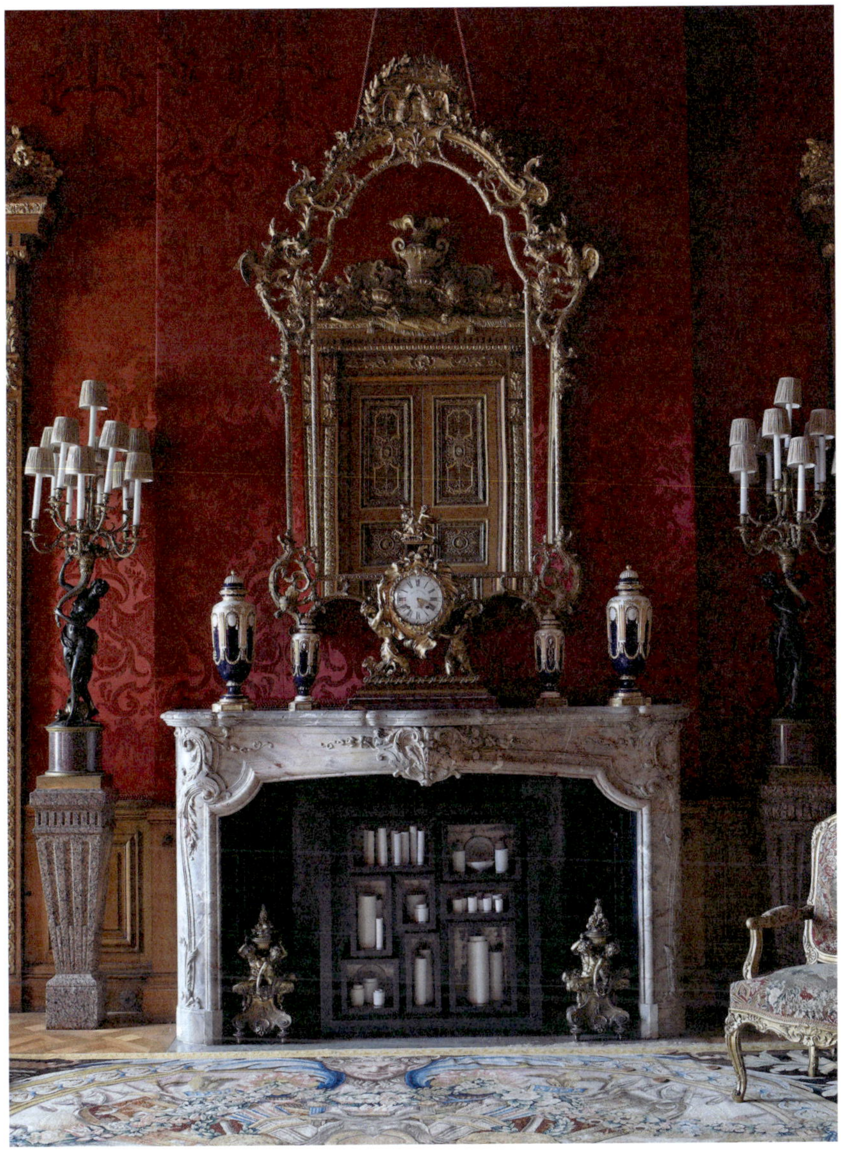

Figure 6.17: Edmund de Waal, *on the properties of fire,* 2012; Exhibition: Edmund de Waal at Waddesdon, 2012. Photo: Waddesdon Image Library, Paul Baker.

[Figure 6.17][42] De Waal has written that he wanted to 'make something that could give the feeling of being on the point of being packed up, ready for transit.' Still and safe, in the fireplaces or in store at Waddesdon, Baron Edmond de Rothschild's boxes resonate with memories of journeys between houses, between depots, between countries – and between generations. I hope the reader can now visualise something of what is going on inside them, when the time comes, as it does each year, to put their contents back on display.

42 This work (48 thrown porcelain vessels, jars and dishes in celadon and white glazes contained in 8 black lacquer, lead-lined boxes stacked inside a black lacquer box) (96.5 × 95 × 40cm) was made as part of the exhibition *Edmund de Waal at Waddesdon*, Waddesdon Manor, 2012; see Edmund de Waal, Rachel Boak and Juliet Carey, *Edmund de Waal at Waddesdon* (Aylesbury: The Rothschild Foundation, 2012), 71. De Waal describes the piece: 'This installation, with is a series of eight balanced boxes lined with lead, has echoes of the stacks of wooden boxes used to transport porcelain; boxes which were in the fireplace when I first visited Waddesdon. I hoped to make something that could give the feeling of being on the point of packed up, ready for transit. Or ready for archiving. Lead, after all is the material to line strong boxes'.